Serverless Web Applications with React and Firebase

Develop real-time applications for web and mobile platforms

Harmeet Singh
Mayur Tanna

BIRMINGHAM - MUMBAI

Serverless Web Applications with React and Firebase

Commissioning Editor: Kunal Chaudhari
Acquisition Editor: Isha Raval
Content Development Editor: Francis Carneiro
Technical Editor: Ralph Rosario
Copy Editor: Shaila Kusanale
Project Coordinator: Devanshi Doshi
Proofreader: Safis Editing
Indexer: Tejal Daruwale Soni
Graphics: Jason Monteiro
Production Coordinator: Nilesh Mohite

First published: April 2018

Production reference: 1040418

Published by Packt Publishing Ltd.
Livery Place
35 Livery Street
Birmingham
B3 2PB, UK.

ISBN 978-1-78847-741-3

www.packtpub.com

`mapt.io`

Mapt is an online digital library that gives you full access to over 5,000 books and videos, as well as industry leading tools to help you plan your personal development and advance your career. For more information, please visit our website.

Why subscribe?

- Spend less time learning and more time coding with practical eBooks and Videos from over 4,000 industry professionals

- Improve your learning with Skill Plans built especially for you

- Get a free eBook or video every month

- Mapt is fully searchable

- Copy and paste, print, and bookmark content

PacktPub.com

Did you know that Packt offers eBook versions of every book published, with PDF and ePub files available? You can upgrade to the eBook version at `www.PacktPub.com` and as a print book customer, you are entitled to a discount on the eBook copy. Get in touch with us at `service@packtpub.com` for more details.

At `www.PacktPub.com`, you can also read a collection of free technical articles, sign up for a range of free newsletters, and receive exclusive discounts and offers on Packt books and eBooks.

Contributors

About the authors

Harmeet Singh is a senior associate working for Synechron with varied experience in UI. He hails from the holy city of Amritsar, India. His expertise includes HTML5, CSS, JavaScript, jQuery, Angular, ReactJS, Redux, Firebase, MongoDB, and Node.js. His interests include music, sports, and adventure.

Harmeet has given various presentations and conducted many workshops on UI development. On the academic front, Harmeet is a graduate in IT and is a GNIIT diploma holder from NIIT, specializing in software engineering.

He can be reached on Skype and LinkedIn at harmeetsingh090.

> *I am really thankful to my colleague Mayur Tanna, whose support and encouragement led me to write this book and kept me motivated throughout the journey of completing this book. I am really thankful from the core of my heart to my girlfriend, Shina, and my best friends Nikhil Nair and Bhawana Dugar for their immense contribution and guidelines.*

Mayur Tanna is a senior big data consultant working with CIGNEX Datamatics. He has worked on various high-value projects with international clients, such as World Bank, and played a key role in creating the architecture of those projects using the latest technologies, including React, Angular, NodeJs, MongoDB, Spring Boot, Firebase, Amazon Web Services, and Google Cloud Platform.

He holds a master's degree in computer applications and has trained a lot of engineering students and freshers through tech workshops.

> *I would like to thank Harmeet Singh, coauthor of this book and my best friend, for his tremendous support and motivation in making this work possible.*
>
> *I want to thank my wife, Dr. Purna, my parents Mr. Ratilal and Mrs. Nirmala, my little child Dhyey, and the rest of my family who supported and encouraged me in spite of all the time it took me away from them.*

About the reviewer

Tejas Suthar, with more than 10 years of working as a software developer, engineer, and product lead, brings a deep understanding of enterprise software, management, and technical strategy to any project. His specialties include microservices architecture, AWS, real-time systems, Alexa Skill Development, enterprise web apps, scalability, education, and open source software. He mostly works on JavaScript development and specializes in Node.Js development with other cutting-edge technologies and frameworks.

Packt is searching for authors like you

If you're interested in becoming an author for Packt, please visit `authors.packtpub.com` and apply today. We have worked with thousands of developers and tech professionals, just like you, to help them share their insight with the global tech community. You can make a general application, apply for a specific hot topic that we are recruiting an author for, or submit your own idea.

Table of Contents

Preface

Realtime applications have dominated the field of web applications for years. Real time isn't limited to only displaying data as soon as it's available; it shows its real power when used with interactive experiences, in which users and systems can instantly communicate with one another. With features such as virtual DOM and declarative views, React proves to be a better fit for such Realtime applications. Firebase makes building and rapid-prototyping these kinds of applications simpler by letting you focus on how the application should behave and look, without getting bogged down in the more tedious parts of Realtime development.

This book will cover the Firebase features such as Cloud Storage, Cloud Function, Hosting, and Realtime Database integration with React to develop rich, collaborative, real-time applications using only client-side code. We can also see how we can secure our application using Firebase Authentication and Database Security Rules. We also leverage the power of Redux to organize the data in the frontend. Redux attempts to make state mutations predictable by imposing certain restrictions on how and when updates can happen. Toward the end of the book, you will have improved your React skills by realizing the potential of Firebase to create real-time serverless web applications.

This book provides more practical insights rather than just theoretical concepts and includes basic to advanced examples—from hello world to a realtime Web Application.

Who this book is for

The idea behind this book is to help developers create real-time serverless applications really faster with React and Firebase. We wrote this book for the developers who want to create **Minimum Viable Product (MVP)** using Firebase to validate a business idea. This book is designed to provide practical knowledge to developers who have basic to intermediate knowledge of HTML, CSS, React, and JavaScript and want to learn more about React, Redux, and Firebase integration. This book is also aimed at developers who don't want to waste their time searching hundreds of tutorials of React, Redux, and Firebase and have everything in one place with real-life examples to get productive quickly. This book is for anyone interested in learning only Firebase.

Lastly, if you want to develop serverless apps and want to know end to end, from designing to hosting, with step-by-step instructions, this book is for you.

What this book covers

Chapter 1, *Getting Started with Firebase and React*, introduces the ReactJS and Firebase features and teaches what you can do with them. It gives a brief detail about setting up a Firebase account and create the demo project with JavaScript.

Chapter 2, *Integrate React App with Firebase*, looks at setting up the React environment and takes a quick look at the JSX and React component methods. It also goes into creating form components in React using JSX and Firebase Realtime Database for our helpdesk application.

Chapter 3, *Authentication with Firebase*, focuses on starting to flesh out the helpdesk application set up in Chapter 2, *Integrate React App with Firebase*, by adding a Firebase Authentication to secure the application with login component.

Chapter 4, *Connecting React to Redux and Firebase*, explores Redux in detail and looks at how and when you need to use Redux in our React app. It will also show you how you can integrate all three—React, Redux, and Firebase—with a sample seat booking application.

Chapter 5, *User Profile and Access Management*, shows you how you can use Firebase Admin SDK, which provides a user management API to read and write Realtime Database data with full admin privileges by creating application admin page.

Chapter 6, *Firebase Security and Rules*, demonstrates how you can secure our database by Firebase Realtime database rules, and it briefly looks at the common database security risks and the checklist to prevent such threats.

Chapter 7, *Using Firebase Cloud messaging and Cloud functions with React*, helps us to send free messages across different platforms: Android, iOS, and web in Realtime. It takes you through how you can run your custom application logic without a server.

Chapter 8, *Firebase Cloud Storage*, covers how you can integrate Firebase cloud storage into your application and see the features and how you can use it.

Chapter 9, *Best Practices*, teaches the dos and don'ts when you are creating a web application with react, Firebase, and redux.

To get the most out of this book

You should have basic programming experience with React, HTML, CSS, and JavaScript to read this book profitably. It is assumed that you know already how **Node Package Manager** (**npm**) works to install any dependencies, and you have a basic idea about ES6 Syntax.

Download the example code files

You can download the example code files for this book from your account at `www.packtpub.com`. If you purchased this book elsewhere, you can visit `www.packtpub.com/support` and register to have the files emailed directly to you.

You can download the code files by following these steps:

1. Log in or register at `www.packtpub.com`.
2. Select the **SUPPORT** tab.
3. Click on **Code Downloads & Errata**.
4. Enter the name of the book in the **Search** box and follow the onscreen instructions.

Once the file is downloaded, please make sure that you unzip or extract the folder using the latest version of:

- WinRAR/7-Zip for Windows
- Zipeg/iZip/UnRarX for Mac
- 7-Zip/PeaZip for Linux

The code bundle for the book is also hosted on GitHub at `https://github.com/ PacktPublishing/Serverless-Web-Applications-with-React-and-Firebase`. In case there's an update to the code, it will be updated on the existing GitHub repository.

We also have other code bundles from our rich catalog of books and videos available at `https://github.com/PacktPublishing/`. Check them out!

Conventions used

There are a number of text conventions used throughout this book.

`CodeInText`: Indicates code words in text, database table names, folder names, filenames, file extensions, pathnames, dummy URLs, user input, and Twitter handles. Here is an example: "Mount the downloaded `WebStorm-10*.dmg` disk image file as another disk in your system."

A block of code is set as follows:

```
constructor(props) {
  super(props);
  this.state = {
  value: props.initialValue
  };
  }
```

Any command-line input or output is written as follows:

```
node -v
```

Bold: Indicates a new term, an important word, or words that you see onscreen. For example, words in menus or dialog boxes appear in the text like this. Here is an example: "Select **System info** from the **Administration** panel."

 Warnings or important notes appear like this.

 Tips and tricks appear like this.

Get in touch

Feedback from our readers is always welcome.

General feedback: Email `feedback@packtpub.com` and mention the book title in the subject of your message. If you have questions about any aspect of this book, please email us at `questions@packtpub.com`.

Errata: Although we have taken every care to ensure the accuracy of our content, mistakes do happen. If you have found a mistake in this book, we would be grateful if you would report this to us. Please visit www.packtpub.com/submit-errata, selecting your book, clicking on the Errata Submission Form link, and entering the details.

Piracy: If you come across any illegal copies of our works in any form on the Internet, we would be grateful if you would provide us with the location address or website name. Please contact us at copyright@packtpub.com with a link to the material.

If you are interested in becoming an author: If there is a topic that you have expertise in and you are interested in either writing or contributing to a book, please visit authors.packtpub.com.

Reviews

Please leave a review. Once you have read and used this book, why not leave a review on the site that you purchased it from? Potential readers can then see and use your unbiased opinion to make purchase decisions, we at Packt can understand what you think about our products, and our authors can see your feedback on their book. Thank you!

For more information about Packt, please visit packtpub.com.

1
Getting Started with Firebase and React

Realtime web applications are said to include the benefits of superfast responses to the user and are highly interactive, which increases the user engagement flow. In this modern web, there are many frameworks and tools that are available to develop Realtime applications. JavaScript is one of the most popular scripting languages that is used for building applications on the web. This book introduces you to ReactJS and Firebase, which you will likely come across as you learn about modern web app development. They both are used for building fast, scalable, and realtime user interfaces that use data and can change over time without reloading the page.

React is famously known as a View in **Model-View-Controller** (**MVC**) pattern and can be used with other JavaScript libraries or frameworks in MVC. For managing the data flow in React app, we can use Flux or Redux. In this book, we will also go through how we can implement redux with React and firebase app.

Redux is the alternative to Flux. It shares the same key benefits. Redux works especially well with React, for managing the state of the UI. If you have ever worked with flux, then it's easy too.

Before jumping into the code, let's refresh our knowledge of ReactJS and see what we can do with Firebase and their features, to know the power of firebase.

Here is the list of topics that we'll cover in this section:

- Introduction of React
- React Component LifeCycle

This will give you a better understanding of dealing with React Components.

React

React is an open source JavaScript library that provides a view-layer for rendering data as HTML to create interactive UI components. Components have been used typically to render React views that contain additional components specified as custom HTML tags. React views efficiently update and re-render the components without reloading the page when your data changes. It gives you a trivial virtual DOM, powerful views without templates, unidirectional data flow, and explicit mutation. It is a very systematic way of updating the HTML document when the data changes and provides a clean separation of components in a modern, single-page application.

The React Component is built entirely with Javascript, so it's easy to pass rich data through your app. Creating components in React lets you split the UI into reusable and independent pieces, which makes your application component reusable, testable, and makes the separation of concerns easy.

React is only focused on View in MVC, but it also has stateful components that remember everything within `this.state`. It handles mapping from input to state changes and it renders components. Let's look at React's component life cycle and its different levels.

Component lifecycle

In React, each component has its own lifecycle methods. Every method can be overridden as per your requirements.

When the data changes, React automatically detects the change and re-renders the component. Also, we can catch the errors in the **Error Handling** phase.

The following image shows the phases of a React Component:

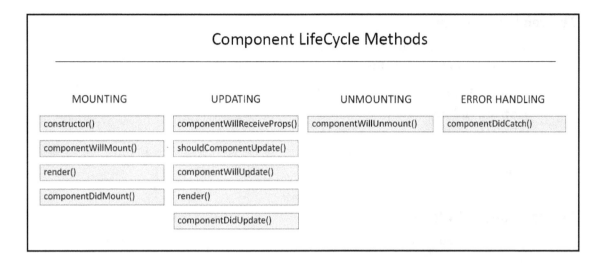

Methods info

Let's take a quick look at the preceding methods.

The constructor() method

The constructor method of React Component gets invoked first when the component is mounted. Here, we can set the state of the component.

Here's an example of constructor in `React.Component`:

```
constructor(props) {
  super(props);
  this.state = {
  value: props.initialValue
  };
}
```

Using `this.props` inside the constructor, we need to call `super(props)` to access and call functions of parents; otherwise, you will get `this.props` undefined in the constructor because React sets the `.props` on the instance from outside immediately after calling constructor, but it will not affect when you are using `this.props` inside the render method.

The render() method

The `render()` method is required to render the UI component and examine `this.props` and `this.state` and return one of the following types:

- **React elements**
- **String and numbers**
- **Portals**
- **null**
- **Booleans**

The componentWillMount() method

This method is invoked immediately before `componentDidMount`. It is triggered before `render()`method.

The componentDidMount() method

This method is invoked immediately after a component gets the mount. We can use this method to load the data from a remote endpoint to instantiate a network request.

The componentWillReceiveProps() method

This method will be invoked when the mounted component receives new props. This method also allows comparing the current and next values to ensure the changes in props.

The shouldComponentUpdate() method

The `shouldComponentUpdate()` method is invoked when the component has received the new props and state. The default value is `true`; if it returns `false`, React skips the update of the component.

The componentWillUpdate() method

The `componentWillUpdate()` method is invoked immediately before rendering when a new prop or state is being received. We can use this method to perform an action before the component gets updated.

This method will not be invoked if `shouldComponentUpdate()` returns `false`.

The componentDidUpdate() method

The `componentDidUpdate()` method is invoked immediately when component gets updated. This method is not called for the initial render.

Similar to `componentWillUpdate()`, this method is also not invoked if `shouldComponentUpdate()` returns false.

The componentWillUnmount() method

This method is invoked immediately before a React Component is unmounted and destroyed. Here, we can perform any necessary cleanup, such as canceling network requests or cleaning up any subscription that was created in `componentDidMount`.

The componentDidCatch() method

This method allows us to catch the JavaScript errors in React Components. We can log those errors and display another fallback UI instead of the component tree that crashed.

Now we have a clear idea about component methods that are available in React Components.

Observe the following JavaScript code snippet:

```
<section>
<h2>My First Example</h2>
</section>
<script>
 var root = document.querySelector('section').createShadowRoot();
 root.innerHTML = '<style>h2{ color: red; }</style>' +'<h2>Hello
World!</h2>';
</script>
```

Now, observe the following ReactJS code snippet:

```
var sectionStyle = {
 color: 'red'
};
var MyFirstExample = React.createClass({
render: function() {
 return (<section><h2 style={sectionStyle}>
 Hello World!</h2></section>
 )}
})
ReactDOM.render(<MyFirstExample />, renderedNode);
```

Now, after observing the preceding examples of React and JavaScript, we will have a clear idea of normal HTML encapsulation and ReactJS custom HTML tags.

 React isn't an MVC framework; it's a library for building a composable user interface and reusable components. React is used at Facebook in its production stages and `instagram.com` is entirely built on React.

Firebase

The Firebase platform helps you develop high-quality apps and focus on your users.

Firebase is a mobile and web application development platform backed by Google. It is a one-stop solution for all your needs to develop high-quality mobile and web applications. It includes various products, such as Realtime Database, Crash reporting, Cloud Firestore, Cloud Storage, Cloud functions, Authentication, Hosting, Test lab for Android, and Performance monitoring for iOS, which can be used to develop and test Realtime applications by focusing on the user's needs, rather than the technical complexities.

It also includes products such as Cloud Messaging, Google Analytics, Dynamic Links, Remote Config, Invites, App Indexing, AdMob, and AdWords that help you grow user base and also increase the engagement of your audience.

Firebase provides multiple Firebase services. We can access each service with the Firebase namespace:

- `firebase.auth()` - Authentication
- `firebase.storage()` - Cloud Storage
- `firebase.database()` - Realtime Database
- `firebase.firestore()` - Cloud Firestore

We'll cover all the preceding services in the upcoming chapters. In this chapter, we will go through the preceding products/services briefly to get a basic understanding of all features of the Firebase platform. In the upcoming chapters, we will explore web-related products which can integrate with React platform, in more detail.

Here's the list of topics that we'll cover in this section:

- Introduction to Firebase and its features
- List of Firebase Features and how we can use it
- Cloud Firestore
- Firebase project setup with JavaScript
- Sample application "Hello World" with Firebase and JavaScript

As you can see, Firebase offers two types of Cloud Database and Realtime Database, and both support real-time data syncing. We can use both of them in the same application or project. Okay, let's go into detail and learn more about them.

Realtime Database

For any Realtime application, we need a Realtime Database. The Firebase Realtime Database is a cloud-hosted NoSQL database that synchronizes the data in Realtime to every connected client. Instead of a typical request-response model, the Firebase database uses the synchronization mechanism that synchronizes the data to all the connected devices within milliseconds. Another key capability is its offline feature. The Firebase SDK persists the data on the disk; so, even if a user loses their internet connection, the app remains responsive. It automatically synchronizes the data once the connection is reestablished. It is supported by iOS, Android, Web, C++, and Unity platforms. We will cover this in detail in the upcoming chapters.

Firebase Realtime Database can scale around 100,000 concurrent connections and 1,000 writes/second in a single database.

The following screenshot shows the list of features on the left, which are available in Firebase, and we have selected the Realtime Database in the database section. In that section, we have four tabs available:

- DATA
- RULES
- BACKUPS
- USAGE

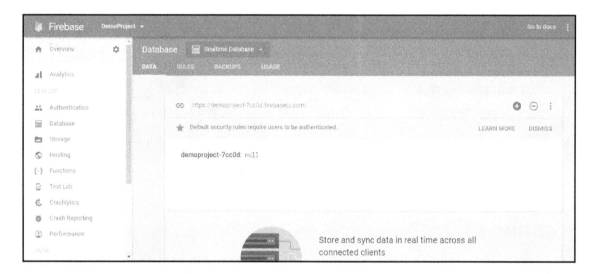

Database rules

Firebase database rules are the only way to secure the data. Firebase provides flexibility and expression-based rules language with JavaScript-like syntax to developers to define how your data should be structured, how it should be indexed, and when the user can read and write the data. You can also combine authentication services with this to define who has access to what data and protect your users from unauthorized access. To validate the data, we need to add a rule separately using `.validate` in the rules.

Consider this example:

```
{
"rules": {
".write": true,
"ticket": {
// a valid ticket must have attributes "email" and "status"
".validate": "newData.hasChildren(['email', 'status'])",
"status": {
// the value of "status" must be a string and length greater then 0 and
less then 10
".validate": "newData.isString() && newData.val().length > 0 &&
newData.val().length < 10"
},
"email": {
// the value of "email" must valid with "@"
".validate": "newData.val().contains('@')"
}
}
}
}
```

Here are some other sample blocks of code for applying rules in the **Rules** tab:

Default: Rule configuration for authentication:

```
{
  "rules": {
  ".read": "auth != null",
  ".write": "auth != null"
  }}
```

Public: These rules give full access to everyone, even people who are not users of your app. They give read and write access to your database:

```
{
  "rules": {
  ".read": true,
  ".write": true
  }}
```

User: These rules authorize access to a node matching the user's ID from the Firebase authentication token:

```
{
  "rules": {
    "users": {
        "$uid": {
```

```
            ".read": "$uid === auth.uid",
            ".write": "$uid === auth.uid"
        }
      }
    }
  }
```

Private: These rule configs don't allow anyone to read and write to a database:

```
{
  "rules": {
     ".read": false,
     ".write": false
  }
}
```

 We can also use REST API with Firebase Secret code to write and update Rules for your Firebase app by making a `PUT` request to the `/.settings/rules.json` path and it will overwrite the existing rules.

Take, for example, `curl -X PUT -d '{ "rules": { ".read": true } }'` `'https://docs-examples.firebaseio.com/.settings/rules.json?auth=FIREBASE_SECRET'`.

Backups

Firebase allows us to save the daily backup of our database, but that is only available in the Blaze plan. It also applies the security rules automatically to secure your data.

Usage

Firebase allows seeing the usage of the database with the help of an analytical chart. It shows us the connections, storage, downloads, and load in Realtime on our firebase database:

Cloud Firestore

Cloud Firestore is also a cloud-hosted, NoSQL database. You might be thinking that we already have Realtime Database, which is also a NoSQL database, so why do we need Firestore? The answer to this question is that Firestore can be considered as an advanced version of Realtime Database that provides live synchronization and offline support along with efficient data queries. It scales globally and lets you focus on developing apps instead of worrying about server management. It can be used with Android, iOS, and web platforms.

We can use both databases within the same Firebase application or project. Both are NoSQL databases, can store the same types of data, and have client libraries that work in a similar manner.

If you want to try out Cloud Firestore while it's in beta, use our guide to get started:

- Go to the `https://console.firebase.google.com/`
- Select your project, `DemoProject`

- Click on the **Database** in the left section navigation and select the **Cloud Firestore** database:

Once we select the database, it prompts you to apply the security rules before creating the database.

Security rules

Before creating a database and collection in Cloud Firestore, it prompts you to apply the security rules for our database.

Take a look at the following screenshot:

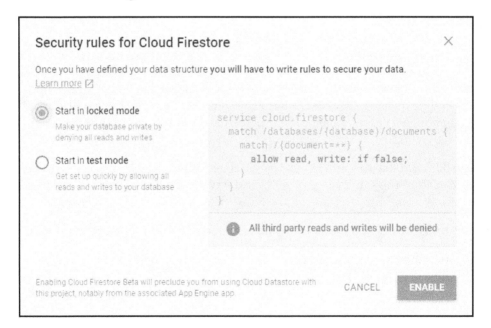

Here are some code example of Firestore rules:

Public:
```
service cloud.firestore {
    match /databases/{database}/documents {
        match /{document=**} {
        allow read, write;
      }
    }
}
```

Users:
```
service cloud.firestore {
    match /databases/{database}/documents {
        match /users/{userId} {
            allow read, write: if request.auth.uid == userId;
      }
    }
}
```

Private:
```
service cloud.firestore {
    match /databases/{database}/documents {
        match /{document=**} {
            allow read, write: if false;
      }
    }
}
```

Difference between Realtime Database and Cloud Firestore

We have seen that both Realtime Database and Cloud Firestore are NoSQL Databases with Realtime capabilities of syncing the data. So, let's see the difference between both of them based on the features.

Data model

Both databases are cloud-hosted, NoSQL databases, but the data model of both databases is different:

Realtime Database	Cloud Firestore
• Simple data is very easy to store. • Complex, hierarchical data is harder to organize at scale.	• Simple data is easy to store in documents, which are very similar to JSON. • Complex and hierarchical data is easier to organize at scale, using subcollections within documents. • Requires less denormalization and data flattening.

Real-time and offline support

Both have mobile-first, Realtime SDKs, and both support local data storage for offline-ready apps:

Realtime Database	Cloud Firestore
Offline support for mobile clients on iOS and Android only.	Offline support for iOS, Android, and web clients.

Querying

Retrieve, sort, and filter data from either database through queries:

Realtime Database	Cloud Firestore
Deep queries with limited sorting and filtering functionality: • You can only sort or filter on a property, not sort and filter on a property, in a single query. • Queries are deep by default. They always return the entire subtree.	**Indexed queries with compound sorting and filtering:** • You can chain filters and combine filtering and sort on a property in a single query. • Write shallow queries for sub collections; you can query subcollections within a document instead of an entire collection, or even an entire document. • Queries are indexed by default. Query performance is proportional to the size of your result set, not your dataset.

Reliability and performance

When we choose the database for our project, then reliability and performance are the most important parts that come to our mind:

Realtime Database	Cloud Firestore
Realtime Database is a mature product: • Stability you'd expect from a battle-tested, tried-and-true product. • Very low latency, so it's a great option for frequent state-syncing. • Databases are limited to zonal availability in a single region.	**Cloud Firestore is currently in beta:** • Stability in a beta product is not always the same as that of a fully launched product. • Houses your data across multiple data centers in distinct regions, ensuring global scalability, and strong reliability. • When Cloud Firestore graduates from beta, it will have stronger reliability than Realtime Database.

Scalability

When we develop a large-scale application, we must know how much we can scale our database:

Realtime Database	Cloud Firestore
Scaling requires sharding: Scale to around 100,000 concurrent connections and 1,000 writes/second in a single database. Scaling beyond that requires sharing your data across multiple databases.	**Scaling will be automatic:** Scales completely automatically (after beta), which means that you don't need to share your data across multiple instances.

Security

As per the security concern, every database has a different way of securing data from unauthorized users:

Source: `https://firebase.google.com/docs/firestore/rtdb-vs-firestore?authuser=0`.

Realtime Database	Cloud Firestore
Cascading rules that require separate validation. • Firebase Database Rules are the only security option. • Read and write rules cascade. • You need to validate data separately using `.validate` in the rule.	**Simpler, more powerful security for mobile, web, and server SDKs.** • Mobile and web SDKs use Cloud Firestore Security Rules, and server SDKs use **Identity and Access Management (IAM)**. • Rules don't cascade unless you use a wildcard. • Data validation happens automatically. • Rules can constrain queries; if a query's results might contain data the user doesn't have access to, the entire query fails.

 As of now, Cloud Firestore is available in beta version; so, in this book, we are only focusing on Realtime Database.

Crash reporting

Crash reporting services help you diagnose problems in your Android and iOS mobile apps. It produces detailed reports of bugs and crashes and also sends them to the configured email address for quick notifications of the problems. It also provides a rich dashboard where you can monitor the overall health of your apps.

Authentication

Firebase Authentication provides a simple and secure solution to manage user authentication for your mobile and web apps. It offers multiple methods to authenticate, including traditional form-based authentication using email and password, third-party providers such as Facebook or Twitter, and using your existing account system directly.

FirebaseUI authentication for web

Firebase UI is completely open source and easily customizes to fit in with your app that includes some set of libraries. It allows you to quickly connect UI elements to the Firebase database for data storage, allowing views to be updated in Realtime, and it also provides the simple interfaces for common tasks such as displaying lists or collections of items.

FirebaseUI Auth is a recommended way to add authentication in Firebase app, or we can do it manually with Firebase Authentication SDK. It allows users to add a complete UI flow for signing in with email and passwords, phone numbers, and with most popular identity providers, including Google and Facebook Login.

FirebaseUI is available at `https://opensource.google.com/projects/firebaseui`.

We will explore more about Authentication in detail in the upcoming chapters.

Cloud Functions

Cloud Functions allow you to have serverless apps; you can run your custom application backend logic without a server. Your custom functions can be executed on specific events that can be emitted by integrating the following Firebase products:

- Cloud Firestore triggers
- Realtime Database triggers
- Firebase Authentication triggers
- Google Analytics for Firebase triggers
- Cloud Storage triggers
- Cloud Pub/Sub triggers
- HTTP Triggers

How does it work?

Once you write and deploy a function, Google's servers start listening to those functions immediately, that is listening for events and running the function when it gets triggered. As the load of your app increases or decreases, it responds by rapidly scaling the number of virtual server instances needed to run your function faster. If the function is deleted, idle, or updated by you, then instances are cleaned up and replaced by new instances. In the case of deletion, it also removes the connection between functions and the event provider.

Given here are the events that are supported by Cloud Functions:

- `onWrite()`: It triggers when data is created, destroyed, or changed in the Realtime Database
- `onCreate()`: It triggers when new data is created in the Realtime Database
- `onUpdate()`: It triggers when data is updated in the Realtime Database
- `onDelete()`: It triggers when data is deleted from the Realtime Database

Here's a code sample of the cloud function `makeUppercase`:

```
exports.makeUppercase =
functions.database.ref('/messages/{pushId}/original')
 .onWrite(event => {
 // Grab the current value of what was written to the Realtime Database.
 const original = event.data.val();
 console.log('Uppercasing', event.params.pushId, original);
 const uppercase = original.toUpperCase();
 // You must return a Promise when performing asynchronous tasks inside a
Functions such as
 // writing to the Firebase Realtime Database.
 // Setting an "uppercase" sibling in the Realtime Database returns a
Promise.
 return event.data.ref.parent.child('uppercase').set(uppercase);
 });
```

 After you write the cloud function, we can also test and monitor our functions.

Cloud Storage

Any mobile or web app will need a storage space that stores user-generated content such as documents, photos, or videos in a secure manner and scales well. Cloud Storage is designed with the same requirement in mind and helps you easily store and serve user-generated content. It provides a robust streaming mechanism for a best end-user experience.

Here's how we can configure Firebase Cloud Storage:

```
// Configuration for your app
 // TODO: Replace with your project's config object
 var config = {
 apiKey: '<your-api-key>',
 authDomain: '<your-auth-domain>',
 databaseURL: '<your-database-url>',
 storageBucket: '<your-storage-bucket>'
 };
 firebase.initializeApp(config);
  // Get a reference to the storage service
 var storage = firebase.storage();

// Points to the root reference
var storageRef = storage.ref();
```

```
// Points to 'images'
var imagesRef = storageRef.child('images');

// Points to 'images/sprite.jpg'
// Note that you can use variables to create child values
var fileName = 'sprite.jpg';
var spaceRef = imagesRef.child(fileName);

// File path is 'images/sprite.jpg'
var path = spaceRef.fullPath

// File name is 'sprite.jpg'
var name = spaceRef.name

// Points to 'images'
var imagesRef = spaceRef.parent;
```

> The total length of `reference.fullPath` must be between 1 and 1,024 bytes, with no Carriage Return or Line Feed characters.
> Avoid using #, [,], *, or ?, as these do not work well with other tools such as Firebase Realtime Database.

Hosting

Firebase provides a hosting service where you can easily deploy your web apps and static content with a simple command. Your web content will be deployed on a **global delivery network (GDN)**, so it will be delivered fast regardless of end-user location. It provides a free SSL for your domain to serve the content over a secure connection. It also provides full versioning and releases management with one-click rollbacks.

Test lab for Android

We test our Android app with a variety of devices running on different Android API versions to ensure that the end user can use our app with any Android device without any issues. However, it is not always possible to make all the different devices available to the testing team. To overcome such problems, we can use Test Lab, which provides cloudhosted infrastructure to test the apps with a variety of devices. It also makes it easy to collect test results with logs, videos, and screenshots. It also tests your app automatically to identify any possible crashes.

Performance Monitoring

Firebase Performance Monitoring is specifically designed for iOS apps' performance testing. You can easily identify the performance bottlenecks of your app with performance traces. It also provides an automated environment to monitor HTTP requests, which helps identify network issues. Performance traces and network data gives better insights on how your app is performing.

The following category of products is used in terms of increasing your user base and also engaging them in a better way.

Google Analytics

Google Analytics is a very well-known product and I think no developer needs its introduction. Google Analytics for Firebase is a free analytics solution to measure the user engagement with your app. It also provides insights on app usage. Analytics reports help you understand the user behavior and hence better decisions can be made regarding app marketing and performance optimizations. You can generate reports based on different parameters, such as device types, custom events, user location, and other properties. Analytics can be configured for Android, iOS, and C++ and Unity apps.

Cloud Messaging

Any Realtime app needs to send Realtime notifications. **Firebase Cloud Messaging (FCM)** provides a platform that helps you send the messages and notifications to the app user in Realtime. You can send hundreds of billions of messages per day for free across different platforms: Android, iOS, and web. We can also schedule the message delivery—immediately or in future. Notification messages are integrated with Firebase Analytics, so no coding is required to monitor user engagement.

Service Workers are supported on the following browsers:

- Chrome: 50+
- Firefox: 44+
- Opera Mobile: 37+

```
// Retrieve Firebase Messaging object.
const messaging = firebase.messaging();
messaging.requestPermission()
.then(function() {
```

```
console.log('Notification permission granted.');
// Retrieve the Instance ID token for use with FCM.
// ...
})
.catch(function(err) {
console.log('Unable to get permission to notify.', err);
});
```

 The FCM SDK is supported only in HTTPS pages because of service workers, which are available only on HTTPS sites.

Dynamic Links

Dynamic Links are URLs that help you redirect users to a specific content location in your mobile app or web application. If a user opens a dynamic link in a Desktop browser, the respective web page will be open, but if a user opens it up in your Android or iOS, the user will be redirected to the respective location in your Android or iOS. In addition, Dynamic Links work across the app; the user will be prompted to install the app if it is not installed yet. Dynamic Links increase the chances of conversion of mobile web users to native app users. Dynamic Links as part of online social networking campaigns also increase app installation and they are free forever.

Remote config

How cool is it to change the color theme of your app without redeploying it on the app store? Yes, it is possible to make on the fly changes to your app through Firebase Remote Config. You can manage the app behavior and appearance through server-side parameters. For example, you can give the certain discount on a specific group of audience based on the region without any redeployment of your app.

Invites

Generally, everybody refers the good apps to their friends and colleagues. We do it by copying and pasting the app links. However, it doesn't always work, due to a number of reasons, for example, the link was for Android, so an iOS user can't open it. Firebase Invites make it very simple to share the content or app referrals via email or SMS. It works with Firebase Dynamic Links to give the users the best experience with their platform. You can associate the Dynamic Links to the content you want to share and Firebase SDK will handle it for you, giving the best user experience to your app users.

App indexing

For any app, it is equally important to get the app installed as well as to retain those users with some engagement. To re-engage the users who have installed your app, App indexing is a way to go. With Google search Integration, your app links will be shown whenever users will search for the content your app provides. Also, App Indexing helps you improve Google search ranking for your app links to show them in top search results and autocompletion.

AdMob

The ultimate goal of the app developer is mostly to monetize it. AdMob helps you monetize your app through in-app advertising. You can have different kinds of ads, such as a banner ad, a video ad, or even a native ad. It allows you to show the ads from AdMob mediation platform or from Google Advertisers. AdMob mediation platform has Ad optimization strategy built to maximize your revenue. You can also see the monetization reports generated by AdMob to define your product strategy.

AdWords

One of the best marketing strategies in today's world is online advertisements. Google AdWords helps you reach the potential customers or app users through ad campaigns. You can link your Google AdWords account to your Firebase project to define the specific target audiences to run your ad campaigns.

Now that we have an understanding of all the products of Firebase platform, we can mix and match these products to solve the common development issues and get the best product out in the market.

Getting started with Firebase

Before we actually use Firebase in our sample app, we have to create our Firebase project through Firebase Console at `https://console.firebase.google.com/`. Opening this link will redirect you to the Google sign in the page where you will have to log in to your existing Google Account or by creating a new one.

Once you successfully log in to the Firebase console, you will see a dashboard like the following screenshot:

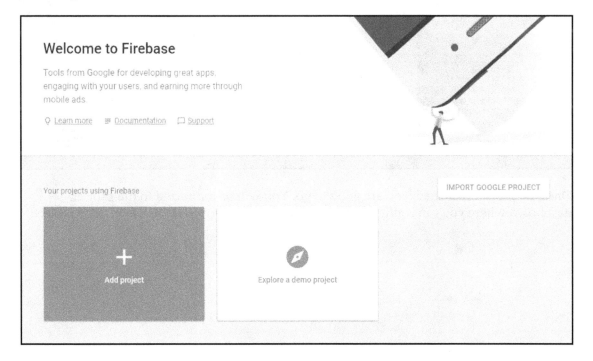

We will create our first project by clicking on the **Add project** button. Once you click on the **Add project** button, it will show a pop-up window asking for the name of your project and the country of your organization. I will call it a DemoProject, set country to the **United States**, and click on the **CREATE PROJECT** button:

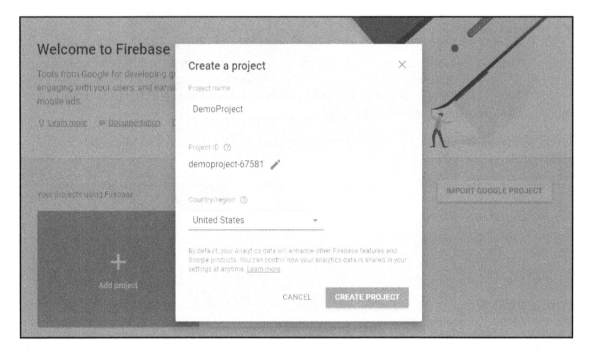

Once the project is created, you are good to go. You will be redirected to the project dashboard where you can configure the products/services you want to use in your project:

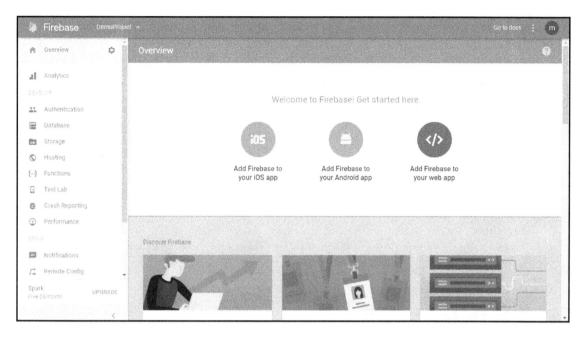

Next, we will look at how we can integrate this Firebase project in a web app. Your web app can be any JavaScript Or NodeJS project.

First, we will create an example with plain JavaScript, and then we will move further and include React.

Now you need to create a directory in your system with the name of DemoProject and inside it, you will create a couple of folders named images, css, and js (JavaScript) to make your application manageable. Once you have completed the folder structure, it will look like this:

To integrate our Firebase project to our JavaScript app, we will need a code snippet that has to be added in our JavaScript code. To get it, click on **Add Firebase** to your web app and note the initialization code it has generated, which should look like the following code:

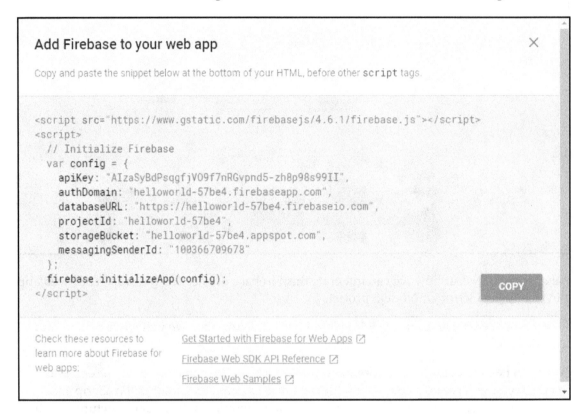

When we start making an application with ReactJS or plain JavaScript, we need to do some setup, which just involves an HTML page and includes a few files. First, we create a directory (folder) called `chapter1`. Open it up in any of your code editors. Create a new file called `index.html` directly inside it and add the following HTML5 Boilerplate code:

- For example, I have created a folder called `DemoProject`
- Create a file called `index.html` in the folder
- In your HTML, add the code snippet we copied from Firebase console:

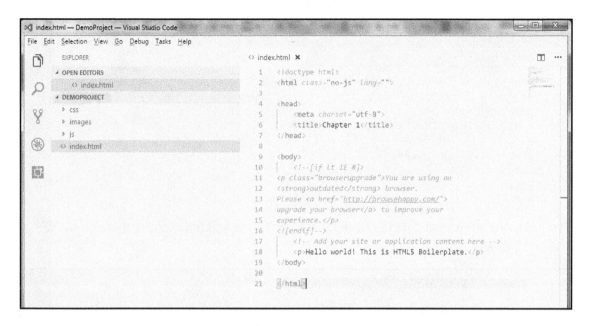

 I prefer and recommend that you use Visual Studio code editor for any type of JavaScript application development over the listed text editors because of its vast array of features.

Now, we need to copy the Firebase code snippet into the HTML:

```html
<!doctype html>
<html class="no-js" lang="">
<head>
 <meta charset="utf-8">
 <title>Chapter 1</title>
</head>
<body>
 <!--[if lt IE 8]>
<p class="browserupgrade">You are using an
<strong>outdated</strong> browser.
Please <a href="http://browsehappy.com/">
upgrade your browser</a> to improve your
experience.</p>
<![endif]-->
 <!-- Add your site or application content here -->
 <p>Hello world! This is HTML5 Boilerplate.</p>
 <script
src="https://www.gstatic.com/firebasejs/4.6.1/firebase.js"></script>
 <script>
```

```
// Initialize Firebase
var config = {
apiKey: "<PROJECT API KEY>",
authDomain: "<PROJECT AUTH DOMAIN>",
databaseURL: "<PROJECT DATABASE AUTH URL>",
projectId: "<PROJECT ID>",
storageBucket: "",
messagingSenderId: "<MESSANGING ID>"
};
firebase.initializeApp(config);
</script>
</body>
</html>
```

The following shows the data in our database, which we will fetch and display on the UI with JavaScript:

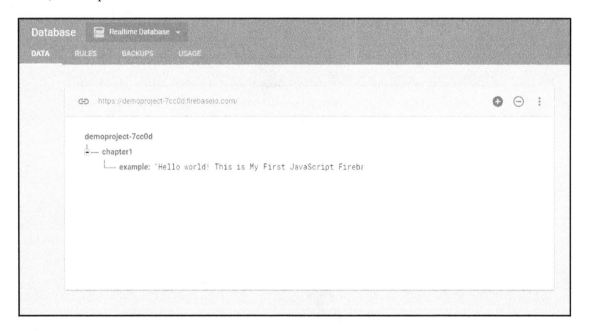

```
//HTML Code to show the message
<p id="message">Hello world! This is HTML5 Boilerplate.</p>
<script>
//Firebase script to get the value from database and replace the "message".
var messageLabel = document.getElementById('message');
 var db = firebase.database();
 db.ref().on("value", function(snapshot) {
 console.log(snapshot.val());
 var object = snapshot.val();
 messageLabel.innerHTML = object.chapter1.example;
 });
</script>
```

In the preceding code, we are using the on() method to retrieve the data. It takes the event type as value and then retrieves the snapshot of the data. When we add the val() method to the snapshot, we will get data to show in the messageField.

Let me give you a brief of the available events in Firebase that we can use to read the data.

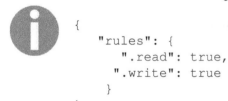

As for now, in Database rules, we are allowing anyone to read and write the data in the database; otherwise, it shows the permission denied error. Consider this as an example:

```
{
    "rules": {
       ".read": true,
      ".write": true
      }
}
```

Firebase events

If you can see the preceding code, we have used the callback function that receives a DataSnapshot, which holds the data of snapshot. A snapshot is a picture of the data at a particular database reference at a single point in time, and if no data exists at the reference's location, the snapshot's value returns null.

value

Recently, we have used this valuable event to read the data from Realtime Database. This event type will be triggered every time the data changes, and the callback function will retrieve all the data including children.

child_added

This event type will be triggered once when we need to retrieve the list of items object and every time when a new object is added to our data as given path. Unlike `value`, which returns the entire object of that location, this event callback is passed as a snapshot that contains two arguments, which include the new child and previous child data.

 For example, if you want to retrieve the data on each new comment added to your post in blogging app, you can use `child_added`.

child_changed

The `child_changed` event is triggered when any child object is changed.

child_removed

The `child_removed` event is triggered when an immediate child is removed. It is typically used in combination with `child_added` and `child_changed`. This event callback contains the data for the removed child.

child_moved

The `child_moved` event is triggered when you're working with ordered data like drag and drop in list items.

Now, let's take quick look at our full code:

```html
<!doctype html>
<html class="no-js" lang="">
<head>
<meta charset="utf-8">
<title>Chapter 1</title><script
src="</span>https://www.gstatic.com/firebasejs/4.6.1/firebase.js"></script>
</head>
<body><!--[if lt IE 8]>
<p class="browserupgrade">You are using an<strong>outdated</strong>
browser.Please <a href="http://browsehappy.com/">upgrade your browser</a>
to improve yourexperience.
</p>
<![endif]-->
<!-- Add your site or application content here -->
<p id="message">Hello world! This is HTML5 Boilerplate.</p>
<script>
// Initialize Firebase
var config = {
 apiKey: "<PROJECT API KEY>",
 authDomain: "<PROJECT AUTH DOMAIN>",
 databaseURL: "<PROJECT DATABASE AUTH URL>",
 projectId: "<PROJECT ID>",
 storageBucket: "",
 messagingSenderId: "<MESSANGING ID>"
};
firebase.initializeApp(config);
var messageLabel = document.getElementById('message');
var db = firebase.database();
db.ref().on("value", function(snapshot) {
 console.log(snapshot.val());
 var object = snapshot.val();
 messageLabel.innerHTML = object.chapter1.example;
});</script>
</body>
</html>
```

Now, open `index.html` in your browser, and let's look at the result:

In the preceding screen excerpt, we can see the database value on `MessageLabel` and JavaScript data representation in the browser console.

Let's extend this example further by taking the input value from the user and save those values in the database. Then, using the events, we will display that messages in the browser in Realtime:

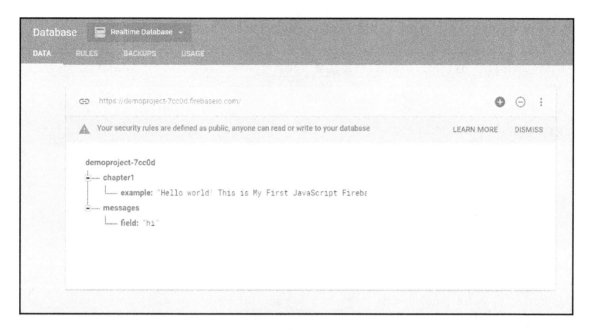

As shown here, I have added a child node `messages` in the database. Now, we will add the form input in our HTML with the **Save** button and at the bottom, we will display those messages list in Realtime when the user submits.

Here's the HTML Code:

```
<input type="text" id="messageInput" />
<button type="button" onclick="addData()">Send message</button>
<h2>Messages</h2>
<p id="list">sdfdf</p>
```

Now, we will create the `addData()` function to get and save the data to Firebase:

```
// Save data to firebase
function addData() {
var message = messageInput.value;
  db.ref().child('users').push({
    field: message
  });
  messageInput.value = '';
}
```

In the next screenshot, I have added some messages to the input text:

Now, we need to display those messages into HTML at the bottom of the messages title:

```
// Update list of messages when data is added
db.ref().on('child_added', function(snapshot) {
var data = snapshot.val();
console.log("New Message Added", data);
  snapshot.forEach(function(childSnap) {
    console.log(childSnap.val());
    var message = childSnap.val();
    messages.innerHTML = '\n' + message.field;
  });
});
```

We have used the `child_added` event, which means whenever any child is added in the messages on node, we need to take that value and update the messages list.

Now, open your browser and note the output:

That looks great. We are now be able to see the message that users have submitted and our data is also getting updated with the new message in Realtime.

Now, let's take a quick look at how our code looks:

```
<!doctype html>
<html class="no-js" lang="">
<head>
 <meta charset="utf-8">
 <title>Chapter 1</title>
 <script
src="https://www.gstatic.com/firebasejs/4.6.1/firebase.js"></script>
</head>
<body>
 <!-- Add your site or application content here -->
 <p id="message">Hello world! This is HTML5 Boilerplate.</p>
 <input type="text" id="messageInput" />
 <button type="button" onclick="addData()">Send message</button>
```

```
  <h2>Messages</h2>
  <p id="list"></p>
<script>
 // Initialize Firebase
 var config = {
    apiKey: "<PROJECT API KEY>",
    authDomain: "<PROJECT AUTH DOMAIN>",
    databaseURL: "<PROJECT DATABASE AUTH URL>",
    projectId: "<PROJECT ID>",
    storageBucket: "",
    messagingSenderId: "<MESSANGING ID>"
 };
 firebase.initializeApp(config);

 var messageLabel = document.getElementById('message');
 var messageInput = document.getElementById('messageInput');
 var messages = document.getElementById('list');
 var db = firebase.database();
 db.ref().on("value", function(snapshot) {
     var object = snapshot.val();
     messageLabel.innerHTML = object.chapter1.example;
    //console.log(object);
 });
// Save data to firebase
 function addData() {
    var message = messageInput.value;
    db.ref().child('messages').push({
    field: message
 });
    messageInput.value = '';
 }
// Update results when data is added
 db.ref().on('child_added', function(snapshot) {
    var data = snapshot.val();
    console.log("New Message Added", data);
    snapshot.forEach(function(childSnap) {
    console.log(childSnap.val());
    var message = childSnap.val();
    messages.innerHTML = '\n' + message.field;
  });
 });
 </script>
</body>
</html>
```

Summary

Our simple Hello World application and Hello World examples are looking great and working exactly as they should; so, let's review what we've learned in this chapter. To begin with, we covered React and Firebase and how easy it is to set up the Firebase account and configuration. We also looked at the difference between Realtime Database and Firestore. Apart from that, we learned how simple it is to initialize Realtime Firebase Database with JavaScript and started building our first Hello World application. The Hello World application that we created demonstrates some of Firebase's basic features, such as the following:

- About Realtime Database and Firestore
- Difference between Realtime Database and Firestore
- Firebase account creation and configuration with JavaScript App
- Firebase Events (value and `child_data`)
- Saving the values into the database
- Read the values from the database

In `Chapter 2`, *Integrate React App with Firebase*, let's build a React application with Firebase. We will explore some more React and Firebase fundamentals and introduce the project that we will build over the course of this book.

2
Integrate React App with Firebase

In Chapter 1, *Getting Started with Firebase and React*, we saw how we can integrate Firebase with JavaScript and created our first sample application, which gave us a brief idea of how Firebase works. Now that you've completed your first web app using JavaScript and Firebase, we'll build the helpdesk application with React and Firebase.

We will start off by setting up the React environment, and then we will take a quick look at the JSX and React component methods. We'll also see how we can create form components in React using JSX and submit these form values in the Firebase Realtime Database.

Here's a list of the points that we'll focus on this chapter:

- React Environment Setup
- Introduction of JSX and React Bootstrap
- Creating a Form With JSX
- Firebase Integration With React
- Save and Read the data from Realtime Database

Setting up the environment

First, we need to create a folder structure similar to our Hello World app, which we made in Chapter 1, *Getting Started with Firebase and React*. The following screenshot describes the folder structure:

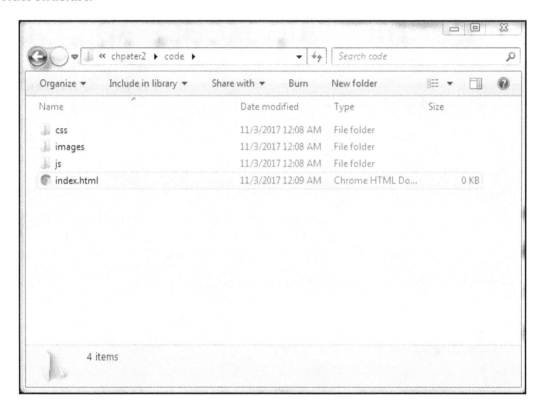

When we start making an application with ReactJS, we need to do some setup, which just involves an HTML page and the reactjs library. Once we have finished creating the folder structure, we need to install both our frameworks: ReactJS and Firebase. It's as simple as including JavaScript and CSS files in your page. We can do this via a **Content Delivery Network** (**CDN**), such as Google or Microsoft, but we will fetch the files manually in our application so that we don't have to be dependent on the internet and can work offline.

Installing React

First, we have to go to `https://reactjs.org/` and see the latest available version that we will use in our application:

As of writing this book, the latest version available is v16.0.0. We will use CDN React packages in this chapter to build our application:

```
<script crossorigin
src="https://unpkg.com/react@16/umd/react.development.js"></script>
<script crossorigin
src="https://unpkg.com/react-dom@16/umd/react-dom.development.js"></script>
```

The preceding versions are only meant for development, and that is not suitable for production. To use minified and optimized production versions, we need to use these production packages:

```
<script crossorigin
src="https://unpkg.com/react@16/umd/react.production.min.js"></script>
<script crossorigin
src="https://unpkg.com/react-dom@16/umd/react-dom.production.min.js"></scri
pt>
```

If you want to use a different version, replace number 16 with the version that you want to use in your app. Let's include development version CDN into your HTML:

```html
<!doctype html>
<html class="no-js" lang="">
<head>
    <meta charset="utf-8">
    <title>ReactJs and Firebase - Chapter 2</title>
    <script crossorigin
      src="https://unpkg.com/react@16/umd/react.development.js">
    </script>
    <script crossorigin src="https://unpkg.com/react-dom@16/umd/react-
      dom.development.js"></script>
</head>
<body>
    <!-- Add your site or application content here -->
    <p>Hello world! This is Our First React App with Firebase.</p>
</body>
</html>
```

Using React

So now that we've got the ReactJS from where we've initialized our app, let's start writing our first Hello World app using `ReactDOM.render()`. The first argument of the `ReactDOM.render` method is the component, which we want to render, and the second is the DOM node to which it should mount (append). Observe the following code:

```
ReactDOM.render( ReactElement element, DOMElement container,[function
callback] )
```

We need to translate it to vanilla JavaScript because all browsers don't support the JSX and ES6 features. For this, we need to use transpiler Babel, which will compile the JSX to vanilla JavaScript before the React code runs. Add the following library in the head section along with React libraries:

```html
<script
src="https://unpkg.com/babel-standalone@6.15.0/babel.min.js"></script>
```

Now, add the script tag with React code:

```
<script type="text/babel">
ReactDOM.render(
<h1>Hello, world!</h1>,
document.getElementById('hello')
);
</script>
```

The `<script type="text/babel">` tag is the one that actually performs the transformation in the browser.

The XML syntax for JavaScript is called **JSX**. We will explore this further in more detail. Let's open the HTML page in our browser. If you see **Hello, world!** in your browser, then we are on track. Observe the following screenshot:

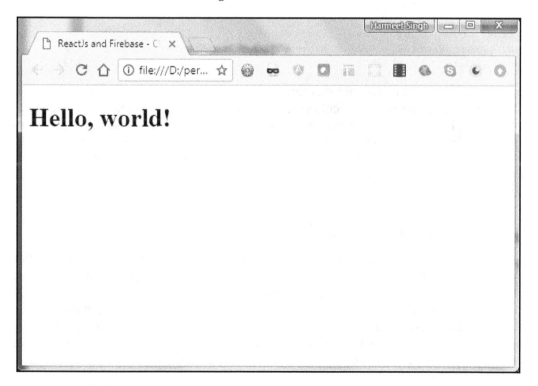

In the preceding screenshot, you can see that it shows **Hello, world!** in your browser. That looks nice. We have successfully completed our setup and built our first Hello World app with ReactJS.

React components

React is based on a modular build with encapsulated components that manage their own state, so it will efficiently update and render your components when data changes. In React, a component's logic is written in JavaScript instead of templates, so you can easily pass rich data through your app and manage the state out of the DOM. Using the `render()` method, we are rendering a component in React that takes input data and returns what you want to display. It can either take HTML tags (strings) or React components (classes).
Let's take a quick look at examples of both:

```
var myReactElement = <div className="hello" />;
ReactDOM.render(myReactElement, document.getElementById('example'));
```

In this example, we are passing HTML as a string into the `render` method that we used before creating the `<Navbar>`:

```
var ReactComponent = React.createClass({/*...*/});
var myReactElement = <ReactComponent someProperty={true} />;
ReactDOM.render(myReactElement, document.getElementById('example'));
```

In the preceding example, we are rendering the component just to create a local variable that starts with an uppercase convention. Use the uppercase convention in JSX to avoid distinguishing between local component classes and HTML tags because JSX is an extension of JavaScript. In React, we can create our React elements or components in two ways: either we can use Plain JavaScript with `React.createElement` or React's JSX. So, let's create our first form component with JSX.

What is JSX in React?

JSX is an extension of JavaScript syntax, and if you observe the syntax or structure of JSX, you will find it similar to XML coding. With JSX, you can carry out preprocessor footsteps that add XML syntax to JavaScript. Though you can certainly use React without JSX, JSX makes React very clean and manageable. Similar to XML, JSX tags have tag names, attributes, and children, and in that, if an attribute value is enclosed in quotes, that value becomes a string. XML works with balanced opening and closing tags. JSX works similarly, and it also helps read and understand a huge amount of structures easier than JavaScript functions and objects.

Advantages of using JSX in React

Here's a list of a few advantages:

- JSX is very simple to understand, compared to JavaScript functions
- JSX code syntax is more familiar to non-programmers
- By using JSX, your markup becomes more semantic, organized, and significant

How to make your code neat and clean

As I said earlier, the structure/syntax is so easy to visualize/notice, which is intended for cleaner and more understandable code in JSX format when we compare it to JavaScript syntax.

The following are sample code snippets that will give you a clear idea of React JavaScript syntax and JSX:

```
render: function () {
return React.DOM.div({className:"title"},
"Page Title",
React.DOM.hr()
);
}
```

Now, observe the following JSX syntax:

```
render: function () {
return <div className="title">
Page Title<hr />
</div>;
}
```

So here we are clear now that JSX is really so easy to understand for programmers who are generally not used to dealing with coding, and they can learn, execute, and write it as HTML language.

React Form with JSX

Before starting on a creating form with JSX, we must be aware of JSX form libraries. Generally, HTML form element inputs take their value as display text/values, but in React JSX, they take property values of respective elements and display them. As we have already visually perceived that we can't change props' values directly, so the input value won't have that transmuted value as an exhibit value.

Let's discuss this in detail. To change the value of a form input, you will use the value attribute and then you will see no change. This doesn't mean that we cannot change the form input value, but for that, we need to listen to the input events, and you will see that the value changes.

The following exceptions are self-explanatory, but very important:

Label content will be considered as a value prop in React. As **for** is a reserved keyword of JavaScript; the HTML for the attribute should be bounded like the HTML for a prop. You'll have a better understanding when you look at the next example. Now, it's time to learn that to have form elements in the output, we need to use the following script, and we also need to replace it with the previously written code.

Now, let's start on building an `Add Ticket form` for our application. Create a `reactForm.html` file in the root and and `react-form.js` file in <strong>js folder. The following code snippet is just a base HTML page that includes Bootstrap CSS and React.

Here's the markup of our HTML page:

```
<!doctype html>
<html lang="en">
<head>
    <meta charset="utf-8">
    <title>Add ticket form with JSX</title>
    <link rel="stylesheet" href="css/bootstrap.min.css">
</head>
<body>
    <script crossorigin
    src="https://unpkg.com/react@16/umd/react.development.js"></script>
    <script crossorigin src="https://unpkg.com/react-dom@16/umd/react-
    dom.development.js"></script>
    <script src="https://unpkg.com/babel-
    standalone@6.15.0/babel.min.js"></script>
</body>
</html>
```

It is always a good practice to load all your scripts at the bottom of the page before your <body> tag closes, which loads the component successfully in your DOM, because when the script is executed in the <head> section, the document element is not available as the script itself is in the <head> section. The best way to resolve this problem is to keep scripts at the bottom of your page before your <body> tag closes, and it will be executed after loading all your DOM elements, which will not throw any JavaScript errors.

 Since JSX is similar to JavaScript, we can't use the class attribute in JSX because it's a reserved keyword in JavaScript. We should use className and htmlFor as property names in the ReactDOM component.

Now, Let's create some HTML layout in this file with bootstrap

```
<div class="container">
  <div class="row">
    <nav class="navbar navbar-inverse navbar-static-top"
role="navigation">
  <div class="container">
   <div class="navbar-header">
    <button type="button" class="navbar-toggle" data-toggle="collapse"
data-target=".navbar-collapse">
    <span class="sr-only">Toggle navigation</span>
    <span class="icon-bar"></span>
    <span class="icon-bar"></span>
    <span class="icon-bar"></span>
  </button>
  <a class="navbar-brand" href="#">HelpDesk</a>
  </div>
  <div class="navbar-collapse collapse">
  <ul class="nav navbar-nav">
    <li class="active"><a href="#">Add Ticket</a></li>
  </ul>
  </div>
  </div>
  </nav>
  <div class="col-lg-12">
  <h2>Add Ticket</h2>
  <hr/>
  <div id="form">
    <!-- Here we'll load load our AddTicketForm component with help of
"form" id -->
  </div>
  </div>
  </div>
  </div>
```

---

[53]

In the above code we have created the navigation and wrapped it into the bootstrap grid classes for responsive behavior of the component.

This is how our HTML looks in the browser.

For our `Add Ticket form` component, we need the following form fields along with the label:

- **Email**: `<input>`
- **Issue type**: `<select>`
- **Assign department**: `<select>`
- **Comments**: `<textarea>`
- **Button**: `<button>`

Also, here's the list of supported events:

- `onChange`, `onInput`, and `onSubmit`
- `onClick`, `onContextMenu`, `onDoubleClick`, `onDrag`, and `onDragEnd`
- `onDragEnter` and `onDragExit`
- `onDragLeave`, `onDragOver`, `onDragStart`, `onDrop`, and `onMouseDown`
- `onMouseEnter` and `onMouseLeave`
- `onMouseMove`, `onMouseOut`, `onMouseOver`, and `onMouseUp`

Let's take a quick look at our form's component code in `react-form.js`:

```
class AddTicketForm extends React.Component {
    constructor() {
        super();
        this.handleSubmitEvent = this.handleSubmitEvent.bind(this);
    }
    handleSubmitEvent(event) {
        event.preventDefault();
    }
    render() {
        var style = {color: "#ffaaaa"};
        return ( <form onSubmit = {this.handleSubmitEvent}>
```

```
   <div className = "form-group">
      <label htmlFor = "email"> Email <span style = {style}> *
</span></label>
      <input type = "text" id = "email" className = "form-control"
placeholder = "Enter your email address" required />
   </div>
   <div className = "form-group">
      <label htmlFor = "issueType"> Issue Type <span style = {style}> *
</span></label>
      <select className = "form-control" id = "issueType" required>
         <option value = ""> -- -- - Select-- -- < /option>
         <option value = "Access Related Issue"> Access Related Issue
</option>
         <option value = "Email Related Issues"> Email Related Issues
</option>
         <option value = "Hardware Request"> Hardware Request</option>
         <option value = "Health & Safety"> Health & Safety </option>
         <option value = "Network"> Network </option>
         <option value = "Intranet"> Intranet </option>
         <option value = "Other"> Other </option>
      </select>
   </div>
   <div className = "form-group">
      <label htmlFor = "department"> Assign Department
      <span style = {style} > * </span>
      </label>
      <select className="form-control" id="department" required>
         <option value = ""> -- -- - Select-- -- </option>
         <option value = "Admin" > Admin </option>
         <option value = "HR"> HR </option>
         <option value = "IT"> IT </option>
         <option value = "Development"> Development </option>
      </select>
   </div>
   <div className = "form-group">
      <label htmlFor = "comments"> Comments
      <span style = {style}> * </span>
      </label>
      ( <span id = "maxlength"> 200 </span> characters max)
      <textarea className = "form-control" rows = "3" id = "comments"
required> </textarea>
   </div>
   <div className = "btn-group">
      <button type = "submit" className = "btn btn-primary"> Submit
</button>
      <button type = "reset" className = "btn btn-default"> cancel
</button>
   </div>
```

```
        </form>
                );
            }
      });
ReactDOM.render( <AddTicketForm /> ,
      document.getElementById('form')
);
```

To apply a style or call an `onSubmit()` function in the attribute value, rather than using quotes (`""`), we have to use a pair of curly braces (`{ }`) in the JavaScript expression. It means that you can embed any JavaScript expression in JSX by wrapping it in curly braces, even a function.

Add this script tag at the bottom of the HTML page after the react libraries

```
<script src="js/react-form.js" type="text/babel"></script>
```

Now, open your browser and let's take a look at the output of our JSX code:

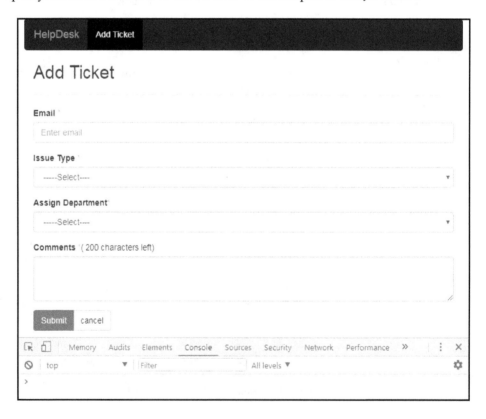

That looks awesome. We can see our form as expected.

> The first character should always be capitalized when you create a component in React. For example, our Add Ticket form component is `<AddTicketForm></AddTicketForm>`.

For the large-scale application, this approach will not be recommended; we cannot put the whole JSX code at one place every time we create form elements. To make our code clean and manageable, we should create a reusable component and just give the reference of that component wherever we need to use it.

So let's see how we can achieve this in our existing code, and we will create one reusable text input component:

```
const TextInput = ({
    type,
    name,
    label,
    onChange,
    placeholder,
    value,
    required
}) => {
    return ( <div className = "form-group">
        <label htmlFor = {name} > {label} </label>
        <div className = "field">
        <input type = {type}  name = {name} className ="form-control"
placeholder = {          placeholder} value = {value} onChange = {onChange}
required = {required}/>
</div>
</div>
    )
}
```

In the preceding code snippet, we created one object that takes some arguments related to the input attribute and assigned those arguments' values to attributes' value:

```
<TextInput
 type="email"
 name="email"
 label="Email"
 placeholder="Enter your email address"
 required={true}/>
```

Now we just need to add the preceding `TextInput` component like this in our `render` method, as you can see in the preceding code, rather than adding the label and input every time in our application; that shows the power of ReactJS.

Using React-Bootstrap

React-Bootstrap is an open source JavaScript framework rebuilt for React. It's similar to Bootstrap where we have ready-to-use components to integrate with React. It's purely reimplementation of Bootstrap framework components to React. React-Bootstrap has no dependency on any other framework, as Bootstrap JS has a dependency on jQuery. By using React-Bootstrap, we can ensure that there won't be external JavaScript calls to render the component that might be incompatible or extra efforts with the `ReactDOM.render`. However, we can still achieve the same functionality and look and feel as Twitter Bootstrap, but with much cleaner and less code.

Let's see how we can create our `Add Ticket Form` component with React-Bootstrap.

First, follow the steps mentioned here to configure React-Bootstrap in your project:

1. Install the React bootstrap npm package by running this below command
    *   npm install --save react-bootstrap

2. If you are using the create-react-app CLI, we don't need to worry about bootstrap CSS; it's already there, we don't need to include.

3. Now by using import keyword we need to add the reference of react-bootstrap components in react application.
    For Example:
    *   import Button from 'react-bootstrap/lib/Button';
        // or
        import { Button } from 'react-bootstrap';

Add Ticket Form with React-Bootstrap

Now, you may be wondering that since we have installed the React-Bootstrap and we have added the reference of React-Bootstrap in our project by using `import` statement, won't they conflict with each other? No, they will not. React-Bootstrap is compatible with the existing Bootstrap styles, so we don't need to worry about any conflicts.

Look at this code for the `Add Ticket` component render method:

```
<form>
    <FieldGroup id="formControlsEmail" type="email" label="Email
    address" placeholder="Enter email" />
    <FormGroup controlId="formControlsSelect">
        <ControlLabel>Issue Type</ControlLabel>
        <FormControl componentClass="select" placeholder="select">
            <option value="select">select</option>
            <option value="other">...</option>
        </FormControl>
    </FormGroup>
    <FormGroup controlId="formControlsSelect">
        <ControlLabel>Assign Department</ControlLabel>
        <FormControl componentClass="select" placeholder="select">
            <option value="select">select</option>
            <option value="other">...</option>
        </FormControl>
    </FormGroup>
    <FormGroup controlId="formControlsTextarea">
        <ControlLabel>Textarea</ControlLabel>
        <FormControl componentClass="textarea" placeholder="textarea"
        />
    </FormGroup>
</form>
```

As you can see in the preceding code, it looks cleaner than the Twitter Bootstrap component, because we can import the individual component from React-Bootstrap rather than including the entire library, such as `import { Button } from 'react-bootstrap';`.

Here's the list of Supported Form Controls:

- `<FieldGroup>` for custom component

- `<FormControl>` for `<input>`, `<textarea>`, and `<select>`

- `<Checkbox>` for checkbox

- `<Radio>` for radio

- `FormControl.Static` (For Static text)

- `HelpBlock`

Now it's up to you whether you want use React-Bootstrap or normal JSX components with Bootstrap styling.

For more detail, check out `https://react-bootstrap.github.io/components/forms/`.

Firebase with React

We are done creating a React form where you can raise the ticket into Helpdesk and save to Firebase. For this, now we need to integrate and initialize the Firebase in our existing application.

Here's how it looks:

Added script tag at the bottom of our HTML:

```
<!--Firebase Config -->
<script src="js/firebase-config.js"></script>
<!--ReactJS Form -->
<script type="text/babel" src="js/react-form.js"></script>
```

Copy the existing Firebase config code from the previous chapter into `firebase-config.js`:

```
// Initialize Firebase
var config = {
apiKey: "<PROJECT API KEY>",
authDomain: "<PROJECT AUTH DOMAIN>",
databaseURL: "<PROJECT DATABASE AUTH URL>",
projectId: "<PROJECT ID>",
storageBucket: "",
messagingSenderId: "<MESSANGING ID>"
};
firebase.initializeApp(config);
var firebaseDb = firebase.database();
```

Also, add `Reactjs Form` into `react-form.js` so that our code looks clean and manageable:

```
class AddTicketForm extends React.Component {
    constructor() {
        super();
        this.handleSubmitEvent = this.handleSubmitEvent.bind(this);
    }
    handleSubmitEvent(event) {
            event.preventDefault();
```

```
        console.log("Email--" + this.refs.email.value.trim());
        console.log("Issue Type--" +
        this.refs.issueType.value.trim());
        console.log("Department--" +
        this.refs.department.value.trim());
        console.log("Comments--" + this.refs.comment.value.trim());
    },
    render() {
        return ();
    }
};
```

Props and state

Before we go into the practical, we should know what is state and what is props in React. In ReactJs, components translate your raw data into Rich HTML with the help of JSX, the props and state together build with that raw data to keep your UI consistent. Okay, let's identify what exactly it is:

- Props and state are both plain JS objects.

- They are triggered by a render update.

- React manages the component state by calling setState (data, callback). This method will merge data into this state and rerenders the component to keep our UI up to date. For example, the state of the drop-down menu (visible or hidden).

- React component props (properties) that don't change over time, for example, drop-down menu items. Sometimes components only take some data with this props method and render it, which makes your component stateless.

- Using props and state together helps you make an interactive app.

Read and Write Form data to Firebase Realtime Database.

As we know, ReactJS components have their own props and state-like forms that support a few props that are affected via user interaction:

`<input>` and `<textarea>`:

Components	Supported Props
`<input>` and `<textarea>`	Value, defaultValue
`<input>` type of checkbox or radio	checked, defaultChecked
`<select>`	selected, defaultValue

In an HTML `<textarea>` component, the value is set via children, but it can be set by value in React. The `onChange` prop is supported by all native components, such as other DOM events, and can listen to all bubble change events.

As we've seen, the state and prop will give you the control to alter the value of the component and handle the state for that component.

Okay, now let's add some advanced features in our `Add Ticket form`, which can help you get the value from user input, and with the help of Firebase, we will save those values in the database.

The Ref attribute

React provides `ref` non-DOM attributes to access the component. The ref attribute can be a callback function, and it will execute immediately after the component is mounted. So we will attach the ref attribute in our form element to fetch the values.

Let's take a quick look at our component after adding the ref attribute:

```
<div>
    <form ref = "form" onSubmit = {this.handleSubmitEvent}>
        <div className = "form-group">
            <label htmlFor= "email"> Email <span style = {style} > *
</span></label>
            <input type = "text" id = "email" className = "form-control"
placeholder = "Enter your email address" required ref = "email" />
        </div>
        <div className = "form-group">
            <label htmlFor = "issueType"> Issue Type <span style = {style}> *
```

```
</span></label>
        <select className = "form-control" id = "issueType" required ref =
"issueType">
            <option value = "" > -- -- - Select-- -- </option>
            <option value = "Access Related Issue"> Access Related
                Issue
            </option>
            <option value = "Email Related Issues"> Email Related
                Issues
            </option>
            <option value = "Hardware Request"> Hardware Request </option>
            <option value = "Health & Safety"> Health & Safety </option>
            <option value = "Network" > Network < /option>
            <option value = "Intranet"> Intranet </option>
            <option value = "Other"> Other </option>
        </select>
    </div>
    <div className = "form-group">
        <label htmlFor = "department"> Assign Department <span style =
{style} > * </span></label>
        <select className = "form-control" id = "department" required ref
= "department">
            <option value = ""> -- -- - Select-- -- </option>
            <option value = "Admin"> Admin </option>
            <option value = "HR"> HR </option>
            <option value = "IT"> IT </option>
            <option value = "Development"> Development </option>
        </select>
    </div>
    <div className = "form-group">
        <label htmlFor = "comments"> Comments <span style = {style
            } > * </span></label>
        ( <span id = "maxlength"> 200 </span> characters max) <textarea
className = "form-control" rows = "3" id = "comments" required ref =
"comment"> </textarea>
    </div>
    <div className = "btn-group"><button type = "submit" className = "btn
btn-primary"> Submit </button> <button type = "reset" className = "btn btn-
default"> cancel </button> </div>
   </form>
</div>
```

Now, let's open the browser and see how our component looks:

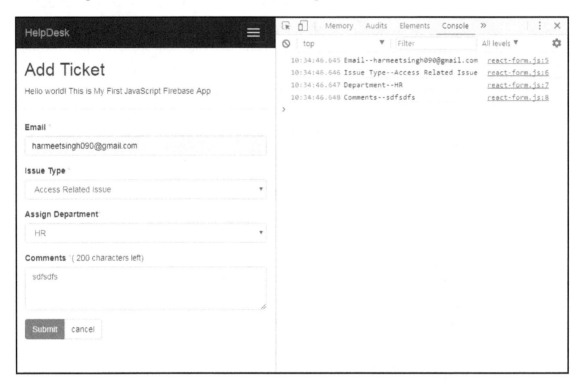

Firebase is working perfectly in our application as you can see the message displayed at the bottom of title "Hello world! This is My First JavaScript Firebase App"; it's coming from Firebase Realtime Database

Also, in the console, you can see the values when we submit the form.

Now we need to save those value into the database:

```
//React form data object
var data = {
   date: Date(),
   email:this.refs.email.value.trim(),
   issueType:this.refs.issueType.value.trim(),
   department:this.refs.department.value.trim(),
   comments:this.refs.comment.value.trim()
}
```

We do this to `Write` the `Form` data object to Firebase Realtime Database;
`firebase.database.Reference` is an asynchronous listener to retrieve the data from
Firebase. This listener will be triggered once on the initial state of that and when data gets
changed.

> We can `Read` and `Write` the data from Firebase Database if we have access
> for that, because, by default, the database is restricted and no one can
> access it without setting up the authentication.

```
firebaseDb.ref().child('helpdesk').child('tickets').push(data);
```

In the preceding code, we used the `push()` method to save the data into the Firebase
Database. It generates a unique key every time a new child is added to the specified
Firebase reference. We can also use the `set()` method to save the data for specified
reference; it will replace the existing data at that node path:

```
firebaseDb.ref().child('helpdesk').child('tickets').set(data);
```

To `Retrieve` the update results when data is added, we need to attach the listener using
the `on()` method, or in any case, if we want to detach the listener on the specific node, then
we can do that by calling the `off()` method:

```
firebaseDb.ref().on('child_added', function(snapshot) {
var data = snapshot.val();
 snapshot.forEach(function(childSnap) {
   console.log(childSnap.val());
    this.refs.form.reset();
   console.log("Ticket submitted successfully");
 });
});
```

However, if we want to read them once without listening to the changes, we can use the
`once()` method:

```
firebaseDb.ref().once('value').then(function(snapshot){
});
```

This is useful when we don't expect any changes in the data or any active listening. For
example, loading the user profile data on the initial load when it gets successfully
authenticated in our app.

To update the data, we have the `update()` method and for deleting, we just need to call the `delete()` method at the location of that data.

 Both the `update()` and `set()` methods return a Promise, so we can use that to know when the write is committed to the database.

Now, let's submit the form and see the output in the browser console:

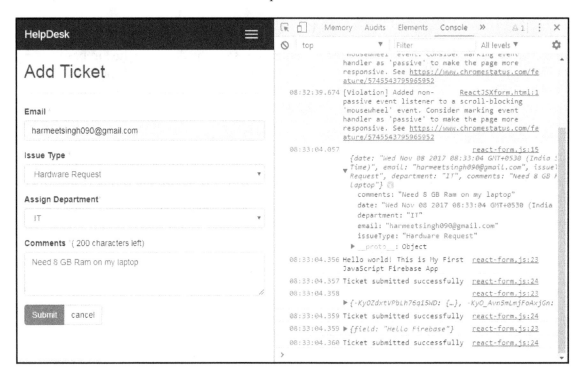

That looks great; now, let's take a look our Firebase database:

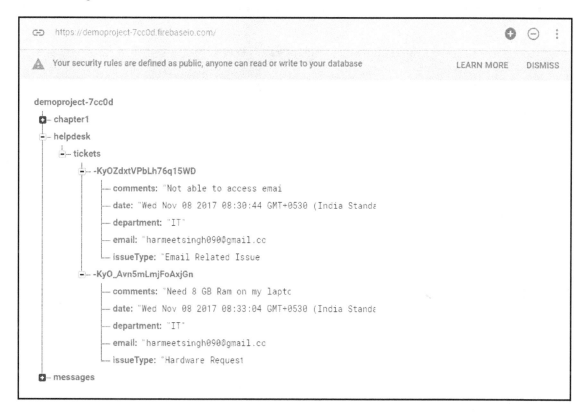

We are able to see the data that we have submitted from the ReactJS form.

Now we'll display this data in a table format; for this, we need to create another React component and set the initial state of our component:

```
constructor(){
    super();
    this.state = {
      tickets:[]
    }
  }
```

Now, using the `componentDidMount()` method, we will call the database by `ref()`, iterate the object, and set the state of the component with `this.setState()`:

```
componentDidMount() {
 var itemsRef = firebaseDb.ref('/helpdesk/tickets');
 console.log(itemsRef);
 itemsRef.on('value', (snapshot) => {
   let tickets = snapshot.val();
   console.log(tickets);
   let newState = [];
   for (let ticket in tickets) {
     newState.push({
       id:tickets[ticket],
       email:tickets[ticket].email,
       issueType:tickets[ticket].issueType,
       department:tickets[ticket].department,
       comments:tickets[ticket].comments,
       date:tickets[ticket].date
     });
   }
 this.setState({
   tickets: newState
 });
 });
},
```

Now we will iterate the state of tickets in a table inside the render method:

```
render() {
  return (<table className="table">
<thead>
<tr>
    <th>Email</th>
    <th>Issue Type</th>
    <th>Department</th>
    <th>Comments</th>
    <th>Date</th>
</tr>
</thead>
<tbody>
 {
   this.state.tickets.map((ticket) =>
     { return (
     <tr key={ticket.id}>
         <td>{ticket.email}</td>
         <td>{ticket.issueType}</td>
         <td>{ticket.department}</td>
```

```
        <td>{ticket.comments}</td>
        <td>{ticket.date}</td>
</tr> )})
  }
</tbody>
</table>
)}
```

Now, the user can view the tickets' list on Realtime whenever a new ticket is added to the database:

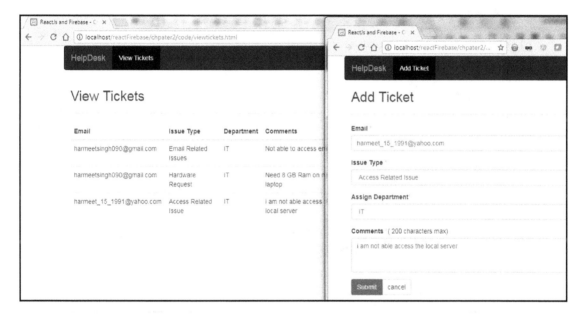

Here's the markup of our HTML page: viewTickets.html:

```
<div class="col-lg-10">
<h2>View Tickets</h2>
<hr>
    <div id="table" class="table-responsive">
        <!-- React Component will render here -->
    </div>
</div>
</div>
</div>
```

This is the list of tickets added in Firebase Realtime Database:

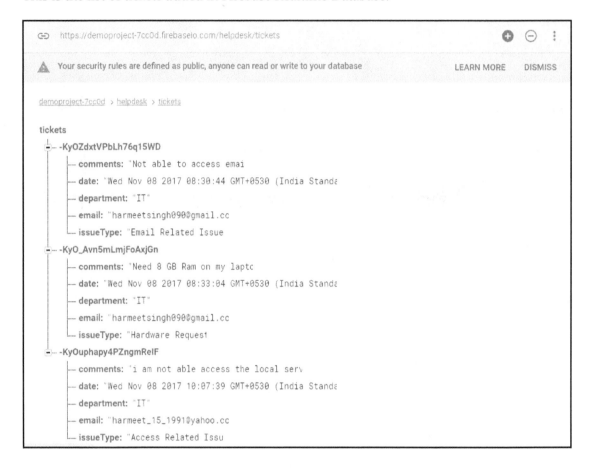

Summary

In this chapter, we saw how JSX plays an important role in making custom components in React as well as making them very simple to visualize, understand, and write. We also saw how props and state play an important role in making components interactive as well as in DOM interaction to get the value from form fields. With the help of `refs`, we can call any public method and send a message to our particular child instance.

Also, we explored the React-Bootstrap components by creating an `Add Ticket form`, which works well on all expected devices as well as on desktop browsers.

In addition, we saw how easy it is to use Firebase Realtime Database with a ReactJS application. With just a few lines of code, we can save the data to the Realtime Database and retrieve the list of tickets from the database in Realtime to make our application Realtime.

In the next chapter, we will do React and Firebase setup on node.js environment and how we can use the Firebase OAuth Providers to add authentication in our application. we'll also explore the react routing for navigation

Authentication with Firebase

In the previous chapter, we learned about how we can integrate Firebase with ReactJS and how we can create a component in JSX. We also saw how we can interact with DOM elements to get the `onSubmit` form values and send them to the Firebase database to store and sync the form data in the cloud. React uses a fast, internal, synthetic DOM to perform to diffs and compute the most efficient DOM mutation for you where your component actively lives.

In this chapter, we'll create a `login` component with React and JSX to secure our helpdesk application with the Firebase authentication feature that allows only authorized users to view and add a new ticket.

Here's a list of the points that we'll focus on this chapter:

- React and Firebase setup with Node.js
- Composite component with React and JSX
- Firebase Authentication Configuration
- Custom Authentication
- Third-Party Authentication with Facebook and Google

React and Firebase setup with Node.Js

Earlier, we created a React application with plain JavaScript; now we need to do the same with React and Firebase setup with using node. For this, we must have Node.js and npm installed in our system; if not, first download the Node.js from https://nodejs.org/en/download/. Once you are done with the installation, run the following command to ensure that node and npm are installed properly:

For node, use this:

```
node -v
```

For npm, use the following:

```
npm -v
```

The output of the command should be as follows:

```
D:\personal\books\javascript\React-FireBase\chapter3>node -v
v8.9.2

D:\personal\books\javascript\React-FireBase\chapter3>npm -v
5.5.1
```

Now we need to install the create-react-app module, which provides the initial and default setup, and gives us a quick start to the React app. Run the following command in your CMD, and it will install the create-react-app module globally (that is, with -g or --global appended to the command):

```
npm install -g create-react-app
or
npm i -g create-react-app
```

Once the installation is done, run the next command in your local directory where we need to create a project; that will generate the quick start project for React with no build configuration:

```
create-react-app <project-name>
or
create-react-app login-authentication
```

This is how our folder structure looks after the installation is done:

node_modules	09-12-2017 01:49	File folder	
public	09-12-2017 01:49	File folder	
src	09-12-2017 01:49	File folder	
.gitignore	09-12-2017 01:49	GITIGNORE File	1 KB
package.json	09-12-2017 01:49	JSON File	1 KB
package-lock.json	09-12-2017 01:49	JSON File	330 KB
README.md	09-12-2017 01:49	MD File	107 KB

Here, we are done with the setup of React; now, we install the firebase npm package and integrate our existing application.

Run the following command to install the firebase npm package:

npm install firebase --save

After installing firebase, create a folder called firebase inside the src folder.

In the src folder, create a file called firebase-config.js, which will host the configuration details of our project:

```
import firebase from 'firebase';

const config = {
  apiKey: "AIzaSyDO1VEnd5VmWd2OWQ9NQuh-ehNXcoPTy-w",
  authDomain: "demoproject-7cc0d.firebaseapp.com",
  databaseURL: "https://demoproject-7cc0d.firebaseio.com",
  projectId: "demoproject-7cc0d",
  storageBucket: "demoproject-7cc0d.appspot.com",
  messagingSenderId: "41428255556"
};
firebase.initializeApp(config);

export default firebase;
```

Similarly, we need to integrate our existing component view ticket and `addTicket` in the node using the import and export keywords, and using the `npm` command, we need to install React and firebase modules and their dependencies.

This how your `package.json` should look like:

```
//package.json
{
 "name": "login-authentication",
 "version": "0.1.0",
 "private": true,
 "dependencies": {
 "firebase": "^4.8.0",
 "react": "^16.2.0",
 "react-dom": "^16.2.0",
 "react-router-dom": "^4.2.2",
 "react-scripts": "1.0.17",
 "react-toastr-basic": "^1.1.14"
 },
 "scripts": {
 "start": "react-scripts start",
 "build": "react-scripts build",
 "test": "react-scripts test --env=jsdom",
 "eject": "react-scripts eject"
 }
}
```

Also, this is how the application folder structure looks after integrating the existing application:

```
▲ LOGIN-AUTHENTICATION
  ▷ node_modules
  ▲ public
    ★ favicon.ico
    <> index.html
    {} manifest.json
  ▲ src
    ▲ add-ticket
      ✿ AddTicketForm.jsx
      JS AddTicketForm.test.js
    ▷ bootstrap
    ▲ firebase
      JS firebase-config.js
    ▷ fonts
    ▲ header
      # header.css
      ✿ header.jsx
    ▲ home
      ✿ index.jsx
    ▲ login
      # login.css
      ✿ login.jsx
    ▲ logout
      ✿ logout.jsx
    ▲ tickets-listing
      ✿ ViewTickets.jsx
      JS ViewTickets.test.js
    ✿ App.jsx
    JS App.test.js
    JS index.js
    JS registerServiceWorker.js
```

Firebase configuration for authentication

Firebase Authentication is a very impressive feature for granting read/write access to your users via security rules. We haven't covered or added security rules in our helpdesk application. Firebase gives us the ability to authenticate with its own email/password and OAuth 2 integrations for Google, Facebook, Twitter, and GitHub. We'll also integrate our own auth system with Firebase to give access to the helpdesk application and allow the user to create an account on our systems.

Let's take a look at the list of firebase providers for authentication and perform the following steps to enable Firebase authentication for our application:

1. Open `http://firebase.google.com` and log in with your credentials
2. Click on the **Authentication** option inside the **DEVELOP** tab on the left section:

In the preceding screenshot, if you can see, we have four tabs that are available in the authentication section, and we have enabled the provider's authentication with the custom Email/Password option, which we can add to the user's tab and Google authentication:

- **Users**: Here, we can manage and add multiple users' email IDs and passwords to authenticate with a variety of providers without writing any server-side code.
- **Sign-in Method**: In this section, we can see the list of providers that are available in firebase. We can also manage the authorized domain, preventing the user from using the same email address and sign-in quota.
- **Templates**: This feature allows us to customize the email templates sent by firebase when users sign up with email and password. We can also customize the template for Password reset, Email address change, and SMS verification.

In this chapter, we'll cover these three authentications:

- Facebook
- Google
- Email/password

Authentication with Facebook

To add a Facebook authentication to our helpdesk application, you need to create an account with Facebook if you don't already have it. Otherwise, we need to log in to the Facebook developer forum at `https://developers.facebook.com/apps`. Once we have logged in, it shows the list of apps and an **Add a New App** button to create a new app ID for authentication. Take a look at this for reference:

Click on the **Add a New App** button; it shows the popup to add the name of the application. Then, click on **Create App Id** that will redirect you to the dashboard of our application:

This is a screenshot of Facebook developer application dashboard. The Purpose of the image is just to show the list of APIs or Products provided by Facebook to integrate with any web application.

For now, we need to select **Facebook Login** to set up:

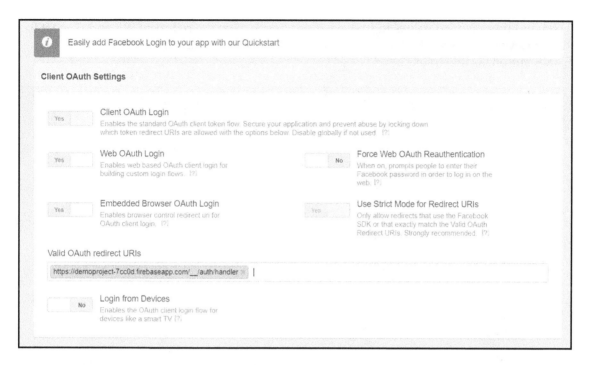

If you can see the preceding screenshot, we need to set up for client OAuth. For this, we first need to enable the **Embedded Browser OAuth Login** feature to control the redirect for the OAuth login, and then copy the valid OAuth redirect URLs, which we can get when we enable the Facebook provider in Firebase.

To enable Facebook authentication in to the Firebase, we need to copy the **App ID** and **App Secret** from the Facebook app dashboard:

Then, put those copied values in firebase input fields, copy the redirect URI, and paste it to **Client OAuth Settings**. Also, enable the facebook authentication and then click on the **SAVE** button, as illustrated here:

This is the last thing we need to do in the Facebook developer forum and firebase for Facebook authentication.

Click on **SAVE**, and note that the status of provider is enabled now:

Now, click on the **Database** on the left-hand side of the section, and go to the **RULES** panel; it should look something like this:

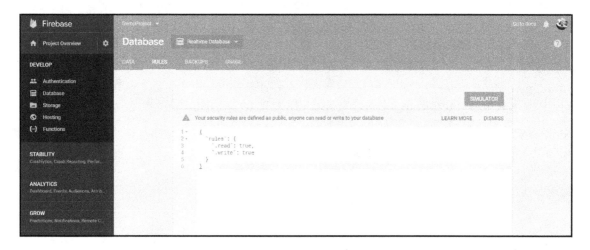

The purpose of the image is to show the list of tabs under the Realtime Database section and under the Rules tab. Here, we can add the security rules for our database to secure our data and with the help of SIMULATOR we can verify whether it's working as expected or not.

Earlier in our application, everyone had the rights to our application and the database to read and write data. Now, we will change the preceding rule configuration so that only authorized users can access the application and write data to our database. Take a look at the given code and publish the changes:

```
{
  "rules": {
  ".read": "auth != null",
  ".write": "auth != null"
  }
}
```

Creating a login form with React for authentication

As we have done with the authentication configuration for Firebase and Facebook and enabled the features for other providers, now we'll create a login form in react to secure the application that always validates whether the user logged in or not; it will redirect the user to the login page. So let's create a login page and also configure the React routing to redirect he user based on the path URL.

Open `firebase-config.js` from the firebase folder and export the following objects with different providers so that we can access those objects across the application:

```
export const firebaseApp = firebase.initializeApp(config);
export const googleProvider = new firebase.auth.GoogleAuthProvider();
export const facebookProvider = new firebase.auth.FacebookAuthProvider();
```

In the preceding code, `new firebase.auth.GoogleAuthProvider()` will provide us with the way to authenticate the user to Google API.

Similarly, new `firebase.auth.FacebookAuthProvider()` will provide us with the way to authenticate the user with Facebook API.

Open `app.js` and add the following code into constructor to initialize the state of the application:

```
constructor() {
super();
  this.state = {
    authenticated : false,
    data:''
  }
}
```

Here, we set the default value of authenticated to be false, because it's the initial state of the application and the user has not yet authenticated with Firebase; the default value of data is empty on the initial state of the component. We will change those states as the user logs in.

First, let's create the `Login` component in `login.js` and set the initial state of that component in `constructor()`:

```
constructor() {
super();
  this.state = {
    redirect: false
  }
}
```

We have set the default value of redirect `false` on the initial state, but that will change whenever a user logs in and out:

```
if(this.state.redirect === true){
return <Redirect to = "/" />
}
return (
<div className="wrapper">
<form className="form-signin"
onSubmit={ (event)=>{this.authWithEmailPassword(event)}}
ref={(form)=>{this.loginForm = form}}>
<h2 className="form-signin-heading">Login</h2>
<input type="email" className="form-control" name="username"
placeholder="Email Address" ref={(input)=>{this.emailField = input}}
required />
<input type="password" className="form-control" name="password"
placeholder="Password" ref={(input)=>{this.passwordField = input}} required
/>
<label className="checkbox">
<input type="checkbox" value="remember-me" id="rememberMe"
name="rememberMe"/> Remember me
</label>
```

```
<button className="btn btn-lg btn-primary btn-block btn-normal"
type="submit">Login</button>
<br/>
<!-- Here we will add the buttons for google and facebook authentication
</form>
</div>
);
```

In the `render` method, we will check the state and redirect the user to a different route `<Redirect>`. It will override the current route in the history stack, like server-side redirects (HTTP 3xx) do.

Here's a list of attributes that we can use with the `Redirect` component:

- `to:String`: A redirect URL that we have also used.
- `to:Object`: A location URL with parameters and other configs, such as state. Consider this example:

```
<Redirect to={{
  pathname: '/login',
  search: '?utm=your+selection',
  state: { referrer: currentLocation }
}}/>
```

- `: bool`: When it's true, redirecting will push a new entry onto the history instead of replacing the current one.
- `from: string`: A URL to redirect from the old URL. This can only be used to match a location inside of a `<Switch>`. Consider this example:

```
<Switch>
  <Redirect from='/old-url' to='/new-url'/>
  <Route path='/new-url' component={componentName}/>
</Switch>
```

 All the preceding `<Redirect>` features are only available in React Router V4.

We have added the JSX for our login form and bound the methods and ref attribute to access the form values. We have also added the buttons for Facebook and Google authentication. Just look at the following code:

```
<!-- facebook button that we have bind with authWithFacebook()-->
<button className="btn btn-lg btn-primary btn-facebook btn-block"
type="button" onClick={()=>{this.authWithFacebook()}}>Login with
Facebook</button>

<!-- Google button which we have bind with authWithGoogle()-->
 <button className="btn btn-lg btn-primary btn-google btn-block"
type="button" onClick={()=>{this.authWithGoogle()}}>Login with
Google</button>
```

In `app.js`, we have configured a router like this:

```
<Router>
<div className="container"> {
this.state.authenticated
?
(
<React.Fragment>
<Header authenticated = {this.state.authenticated}/>
<Route path="/" render={() => (<Home userInfo = {this.state.data} />)} />
<Route path="/view-ticket" component={ViewTicketTable}/>
<Route path="/add-ticket" component={AddTicketForm}/>
</React.Fragment>
)
:
(
<React.Fragment>
<Header authenticated = {this.state.authenticated}/>
<Route exact path="/login" component={Login}/>
</React.Fragment>
)
}
</div>
</Router>
```

In the preceding code, we are using React Router version 4, which is a fully rewritten router for react package. In the previous version of React router, they have used a very difficult configuration, which will be difficult to understand, and also, we need to create a separate component to manage the layout. In Router V4, everything works as a component.

In React router V4, we need to import from react-router-dom, not from react-router, as we do in V3. The `<Router>` component and all other subcomponents get rendered if the route path matches.

Using the `<React.Fragment>` tag, we can wrap any JSX component without adding another node into the DOM.

 In V4 react router, there is no more `<IndexRoute>`; using `<Route exact>` will do the same thing.

Now we'll change the header component where we have navigation and add the link to login and logout:

```
class Header extends Component {
render() {
 return (
 <div className="navbar navbar-inverse firebase-nav" role="navigation">
 {
 this.props.authenticated
 ?
 (
 <React.Fragment>
 <ul className="nav navbar-nav">
 <li className="active"><Link to="/">Home</Link></li>
 <li><Link to="/view-ticket">Tickets</Link></li>
 <li><Link to="/add-ticket">Add new ticket</Link></li>
 </ul>
 <ul className="nav navbar-nav navbar-right">
 <li><Link to="/logout">Logout</Link></li>
 </ul>
 </React.Fragment>
 ) : (
 <React.Fragment>
 <ul className="nav navbar-nav navbar-right">
 <li><Link to="/login">Register/Login</Link></li>
 </ul>
 </React.Fragment>
 )
 }
 </div>
 );
 }
}
```

It's necessary to use this if we are working with the React router. Let's add `<link>` in our navigation instead of the `<a>` tag and replace the `href` attribute with `to`. In V4, we can also use `<NavLink>`; it works the same as `<Link>`, but gives us the way to add extra styling. Look at this code:

```
<li><NavLink to="/view-ticket/" activeClassName="active"
activeStyle={{fontWeight: 'bold', color: red'}} exact
strict>Tickets</NavLink></li>
```

Based on the authentication, we'll update the navigation with login and a logout link.

Start the server again by running the following command in Command Prompt:

```
npm start
```

Once your server is started, open the browser and take a quick look:

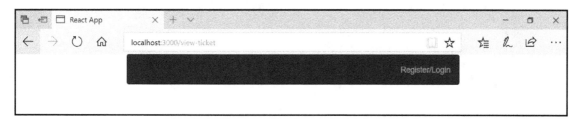

If you just take a look at the preceding screen excerpt and note the address bar, I have tried to open another URL to view the tickets, but it's not showing anything except header login link; so now, if we click on **Login**, it will render the login form. Refer to the following screenshot; it should look like this:

It's amazing that our login form looks great, as expected.

> *For more information about react router, you can go through* `https://reacttraining.com/react-router/web/api`.

Authentication with Facebook

The `onClick` of each of these buttons will point to three functions that will authenticate the user. The Facebook authentication method, which will handle our authentication with Firebase, will look like this:

```
authWithFacebook(){
console.log("facebook");
firebaseApp.auth().signInWithPopup(facebookProvider).then((result,error)=>{
if(error){
   console.log("unable to sign in with facebook");
}
else{
   this.setState({redirect:true})
}}).catch((error)=>{
      ToastDanger(error.message);
   })
}
```

Here, we call the `signInWithPopup()` method from the firebase `auth` module and pass the facebook provider.

> *To display the error messages on UI, we are using React Toaster module and passing those messages into it (don't forget to install and import the React Toaster module before using it). We also need to bind* `authWithFacebook()` *methods into the constructor.*

```
npm install --save react-toastr-basic
```

TIP

```
// In app.js import the container
import ToastrContainer from 'react-toastr-basic';

//Inside the render method
<ToastrContainer />
```

```
constructor() {
 super();
 this.authWithFacebook = this.authWithFacebook.bind(this);
 this.state = {
  redirect: false,
  data:null
 }}
```

Now, when we click on the **Login with Facebook** button, it will open a popup that gives us the option to sign in with a Facebook account, as shown:

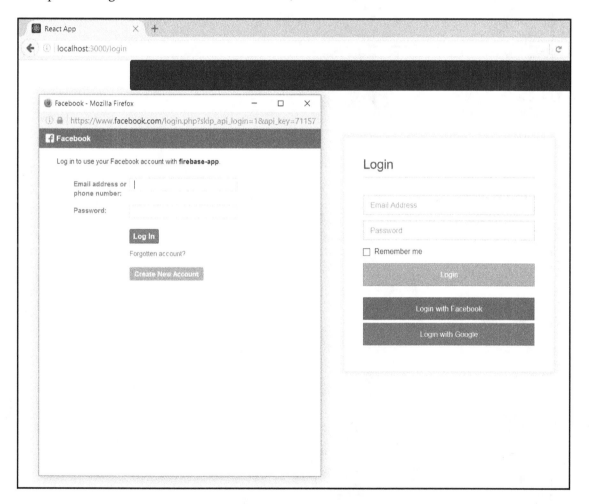

`signInWithPopup()` has a promise API that allows us to call `.then()` on it and pass in a callback. This callback will be provided with a result object that contains, among other things, an object called `user` that has all the information about the user who has just successfully signed in—including their name, email, and user photo URL. We will store this object inside of the state using `setState()` and display the name, email, and photo of the user on UI:

Authentication with Google

In the same way, we can configure Google authentication in our application; just add the following code into the `authWithGoogle()` method, and it will open the popup for login with Google:

```
authWithGoogle(){
console.log("Google");
googleProvider.addScope('profile');
googleProvider.addScope('email');
firebaseApp.auth().signInWithPopup(googleProvider).then((result,error)=>{
  if(error){
    console.log("unable to sign in with google");
  }
  else{
    this.setState({redirect:true,data:result.user})
}}).catch((error)=>{
    ToastDanger(error.message);
  })
}
```

As you can see, I have added the additional OAuth 2.0 scopes that we want to request from the auth provider. To add a scope, call add the scope. We can also define the language code with `firebase.auth().languageCode = 'pt';`. If we want to send a specific custom parameter with the request, we can call the `setCustomParamter()` method. Consider this example:

```
provider.setCustomParameters({
  'login_hint': 'admin'
});
```

So, once you click on the **Login with Google** button, it will trigger the popup to authenticate with Google:

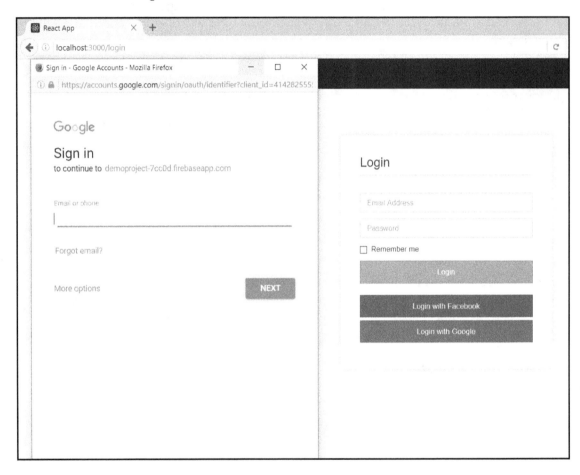

So if you are already logged in and try to log in with the same email ID with different providers, it throws errors, as illustrated:

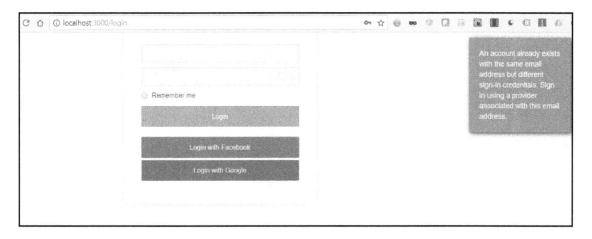

Okay, so now let's see how we can handle these types of errors.

Handling account exists errors

Consider that we have enabled the **One account per email address** option in firebase settings. As you can see in the preceding screenshot when we tried to log in with the provider (Google) with an email that already exists in firebase with a different provider (such as Facebook), it throws the mentioned error—`auth/account-exists-with-different-credential`—which we can see in the preceding screenshot. To handle this error and complete the sign into the selected provider, the user has to sign in first to the existing provider (Facebook) and then link to the former AuthCredential (with Google ID token). After rewriting the `authWithFacebook()` method, this is how our code looks:

```
if (error.code === 'auth/account-exists-with-different-credential') {
// Step 2.
var pendingCred = error.credential;
// The provider account's email address.
var email = error.email;
// Get registered providers for this email.
firebaseApp.auth().fetchProvidersForEmail(email).then(function(providers)
{
// Step 3.
// If the user has several providers,
// the first provider in the list will be the "recommended" provider to
use.
if (providers[0] === 'password') {
// Asks the user his password.
// In real scenario, you should handle this asynchronously.
var password = promptUserForPassword(); // TODO: implement
```

```
promptUserForPassword to open the dialog to get the user entered password.
  firebaseApp.auth().signInWithEmailAndPassword(email,
password).then(function(user) {
  // Step 4.
  return user.link(pendingCred);
  }).then(function() {
  // Google account successfully linked to the existing Firebase user.
  });
  }
})}
```

To know more about the list of error codes, visit https://firebase.google.com/docs/
reference/js/firebase.auth.Auth#signInWithPopup.

Managing the Login across Refresh

As of right now, every time we refresh the page, our application forgets that the user was already logged in. However, Firebase has an event listener—onAuthStateChange()—that can actually check every single time the application loads to see whether the authentication state is changed or not, whether the user was already signed in the last time they visited the app. If it's true, then you can automatically sign them back in.

We'll write this method inside our componentDidMount() in app.js. Just look at the following code:

```
componentWillMount() {
  this.removeAuthListener = firebase.auth().onAuthStateChanged((user)
  =>{
   if(user){
    console.log("App user data",user);
    this.setState({
      authenticated:true,
      data:user.providerData
    })
  }
  else{
    this.setState({
      authenticated:false,
      data:''
})}
})}
```

Also, in `componentWillUnmount()`, we will remove that listener to avoid memory leaks:

```
componentWillUnmount(){
    this.removeAuthListener();
}
```

Now if you refresh the browser, it will not affect the state of the application; it remains the same if you already logged in.

After logging in with Facebook API or any other, we need to display user information in the UI. For this, if you look at that the router component again, we are sending this user information into the Home component with `userInfo` props:

```
<Route path="/" render={() => (<Home userInfo = {this.state.data} />)} />
```

In the `Home` component's render method, we'll iterate the `userInfo` props that hold the user data who successfully logged in to the system:

```
render() {
var userPhoto = {width:"80px",height:"80px",margintop:"10px"};
return (
<div>
{
this.props.userInfo.map((profile)=> {
return (
<React.Fragment key={profile.uid}>
<h2>{ profile.displayName } - Welcome to Helpdesk Application</h2>
<div style={userPhoto}>
<img src = { profile.photoURL } alt="user"/>
<br/>
<span><b>Eamil:</b></span> {profile.email }
</div>
</React.Fragment>
)})
}
</div>
)}
```

In the `Logout()` method, we will simply call the `signOut()` method from firebase auth; by using the Promise API, we remove the user data from our application's state. With `this.state.data` now equal to null, the user will see the **login** link instead of the **Logout** button. It should look like this:

```
constructor() {
  super();
   this.state = {
      redirect: false,
```

```
    data:''
  }
}
componentWillMount(){
  firebaseApp.auth().signOut().then((user)=>{
    this.setState({
      redirect:true,
      data: null
    })
})}
render() {
if(this.state.redirect === true){
return <Redirect to = "/" />
}
return (
<div
style={{textAlign:"center",position:"absolute",top:"25%",left:"50%"}}>
<h4>Logging out...</h4>
</div>);
}
```

Authentication with email and password

In Firebase, we can also integrate your own auth systems with Firebase Authentication to give users access to data without forcing them to create an account using third-party APIs of your existing systems. Firebase also allows for anonymous auth sessions, which are typically used to save small amounts of data while waiting for a client to authenticate with a permanent `auth` method. We can configure this anonymous session with last days, weeks, months, or even years until the user logs in with a permanent `login` method or clears their browser cache. For example, a shopping cart application can create an anonymous auth session for every user who adds something to their cart while doing a shopping. The shopping cart app will prompt the user to create an account for checkout; at that point, the cart will be persisted to the new user's account, and the anonymous session will be destroyed.

Supported types of Auth state persistence

We can use one of the three types of the persistence that are available in firebase on specified Firebase Authentication `instance(.auth())` based on your application or user's requirements:

Auth instance	Value	Description
`firebase.auth.Auth.Persistence.LOCAL`	'local'	It Indicates that the state will be persisted even if we closed the browser window or the activity is destroyed in React Native. For this, explicit sign out is needed to clear that state.
`firebase.auth.Auth.Persistence.SESSION`	'session'	In this scenario, the state will persist only to the current session or tab and will be cleared when the tab or window is closed in which the user has authenticated.
`firebase.auth.Auth.Persistence.NONE`	'none'	When we specify this, it means that the state will be only stored in the memory and will be cleared when window or application is refreshed.

Consider this example:

```
firebaseApp.auth().setPersistence('session')
.then(function() {
// Auth state is now persisted in the current
// session only. If user directly close the browser window without doing
signout then it clear the existing state
// ...
// New sign-in will be persisted with session.
return firebase.auth().signInWithEmailAndPassword(email, password);
})
.catch(function(error) {
// Handle Errors here.
});
```

Let's create a function with the name of `authWithEmailPassword()` and add the following code to it:

```
const email = this.emailField.value
const password = this.passwordField.value;
firebaseApp.auth().fetchProvidersForEmail(email).then((provider)=>{
 if(provider.length === 0){
 //Creating a new user
 return firebaseApp.auth().createUserWithEmailAndPassword(email,password);
 } else if(provider.indexOf("password") === -1){
 this.loginForm.reset();
 ToastDanger('Wrong Password. Please try again!!')
 } else {
 //signin user
 return firebaseApp.auth().signInWithEmailAndPassword(email,password);
 }}).then((user) => {
 if(user && user.email){
 this.loginForm.reset();
 this.setState({redirect: true});
 }})
 .catch((error)=>{
 console.log(error);
 ToastDanger(error.message);
 })
```

In the preceding code, first, we are getting the values from the form. When the user clicks on the submit button, then with the help of `fetchProvidersForEmail(email)`, we are validating whether the email exists in our current firebase system; if not, it will create a new user using the `createUserWithEmailAndPassword()` method. If it returns true, then we will validate the password; if the user entered the wrong password, it will prompt the user with **Wrong password**, otherwise sign them in using the same method—`signInWithEmailAndPassword()`—and we'll update the state of the component by redirecting true.

When we'll create a new user in the `createUserWithEmailAndPassword()` method, it returns the following error code:

- **auth/email-already-in-use**
- **auth/invalid-email**
- **auth/operation-not-allowed** (if email/password accounts are not enabled in Firebase Console.)
- **auth/weak-password** (if the password is not strong enough.)

When we'll fetch the provider based on the email
with `fetchProvidersForEmail(email)`, then it returns the following error code:

- **auth/invalid-email** (If a user entered the invalid email)

To read the list of more auth methods and error codes, refer to `https://firebase.google.com/docs/reference/js/firebase.auth.Auth`.

We can also use the following firebase methods in our application to manipulate the user:

```
var currentUser = firebase.auth().currentUser;
currentUser.updateProfile({
 displayName: "Harmeet Singh",
 photoURL: "http://www.liferayui.com/g/200/300"
});
currentUser.sendPasswordResetEmail("harmeetsingh090@gmail.com"); // Sends a
temporary password
// Re-authentication is necessary for email, password and delete functions
var credential = firebase.auth.EmailAuthProvider.credential(email,
password);
currentUser.reauthenticate(credential);
currentUser.updateEmail("harmeetsingh090@gmail.com");
currentUser.updatePassword("D@#Log123");
currentUser.delete();
```

After successful login, we'll be redirected to an application dashboard page, and we'll be able to see the full navigation where we can add and view the tickets:

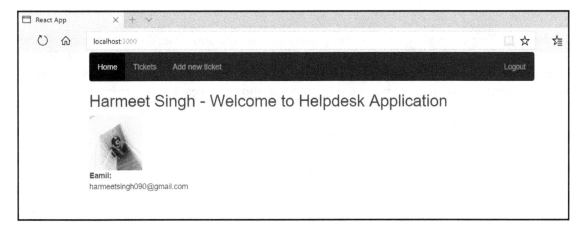

Now if you click on the **logout** button, nothing will happen, because we have not yet created any `logout` component. So in the logout button, what we need to do is simply call the `signOut()` method of the firebase:

```
class Logout extends Component {
  constructor(props) {
  super();
   this.state = {
      redirect: props.authenticated,
      data:''
  }}
  componentWillMount(){
    firebaseApp.auth().signOut().then((user)=>{
      this.setState({
          redirect:true,
          data: null
    })
})}
  render() {
  if(this.state.redirect === true){
     return <Redirect to = "/" />
  }
  return (
  <div
 style={{textAlign:"center",position:"absolute",top:"25%",left:"50%"}}>
     <h4>Logging out...</h4>
  </div>
  );
 }}
```

In the preceding code, we created a component and set the state based on the passing value in the component props (authenticated); then, inside component lifecycle hook method `componentWillMount()`, we called the `firebaseApp.auth().signout()` method that signs out the user redirects them to the login page, and removes the data from the state.

Summary

In this chapter, we saw how we can make our application secure from unknown users with the help of firebase authentication system. We also saw how we can configure the React - Firebase application in node environment as well as how to create a login form in React and integrate the Firebase Authentication Sign-in method in React, such as Google, Facebook, and Email/Password. Similarly, we can integrate the other Authentication sign-in methods in your application.

We also covered handling the authentication errors based on the firebase auth error codes that help us perform an action in the application. To `Persist` the auth state, we can use `firebaseApp.auth().setPersistence('session')`, the method that allows us to maintain the firebase auth state.

In the next chapter, we will explore the power of Redux and create a realtime ticket booking application with React, Redux and Firebase.

Connecting React to Redux and Firebase

In Chapter 3, *Authentication with Firebase*, we saw how React components can be built and how they manage their own state. In this chapter, we will take a look at how to efficiently manage the application state. We will explore Redux in detail and see how and when we need to use Redux in our React app. We will also see how we can integrate all three—React, Redux, and Firebase—with a sample seat booking application. It will be a general seat booking app, and it can be used as any seat booking, such as bus seat booking, a stadium seat booking, or a theater seat booking, with some minor changes in the data structure.

Here's a list of the topics we will cover in this chapter:

- React setup with React Starter Kit
- Integration of Firebase Realtime Database and React
- Redux
- Integration of React, Redux, and Firebase Realtime Database
- Seat Booking Application covering all the above concepts practically

Let's set up our development environment.

 To set up the React development environment, you will need to have node version 6.0 or greater.

React setup

To set up our development environment, the first step will be the React setup. There are different options available to install React. If you already have an existing app and want to add React, you can install it using a package manager such as npm using this command:

```
npm init
npm install --save react react-dom
```

However, if you are starting a new project, the easiest way to get started is with the React Starter Kit. Just go to the Command Prompt and execute the following command to install the React Starter kit:

```
npm install -g create-react-app
```

This command will install and set up the local development environment by downloading all the required dependencies. There are a number of benefits to have your development environment with node, such as optimized production builds, installing libraries using simple npm or yarn commands, and such.

Once you have it installed, you can create your first app using the given command:

```
create-react-app seat-booking
```

It will create a frontend application and will not include any backend logic or integration. It is just frontend and hence you can integrate it with any backend technology or in your existing project.

The preceding command will take a while to download all dependencies and create the project, so keep patience.

Once the project is created, just go into that folder and run the server:

```
cd seat-booking
npm start
```

Once the server is started, you can access the application at http://localhost:3000.

The start kit is the best way to start with React. However, if you are an advanced user, you can manually configure your project by adding React dependencies using the following commands:

```
npm init
npm install --save react react-dom
```

For this sample seat booking app, we will use the `create-react-app` command.

The project structure will look as follows if you see it in the Visual Code editor:

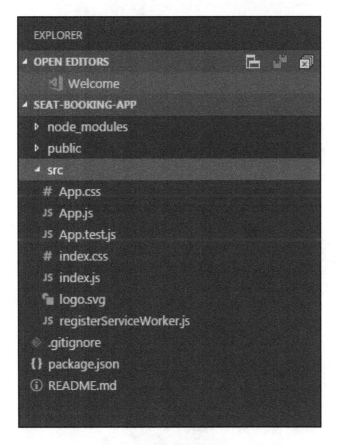

The created app structure is good enough to get started, but for our seat booking app, we will need to organize our source code in a better package structure.

So, we will create the different folders for actions, components, containers, and reducers, as shown in the following screenshot. For now, just focus on the `components` folder, because in that, we will put our React components. The rest of the folders are related to Redux, which we will see in the Redux section:

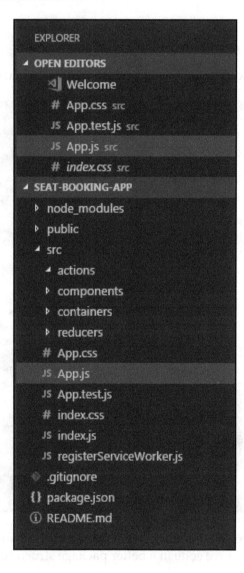

It is very important to identify the components at the start of application development so that you can have a better code structure.

Just to start with, we will have the following React components in our seat booking application:

- `Seat`: Seat Object and basic building block of the application
- `SeatRow`: It represents a row of seats
- `SeatList`: It represents the list of all seats
- `Cart`: It represents the cart that will have information on selected seats

Note that the design of components depends on the application complexity and data structure of the application.

Let's start with our first component called Seat. This will be under the `components` folder.

`components/Seat.js`:

```
import React from 'react'
import PropTypes from 'prop-types'

const Seat = ({ number, price, status }) => (
  <li className={'seatobj ' + status} key={number.toString()}>
    <input type="checkbox" disabled={status === "booked" ? true : false}
id={number.toString()} onClick={handleClick}/>
    <label htmlFor={number.toString()}>{number}</label>
  </li>
)
const handleClick = (event) => {
  console.log("seat selected " + event.target.checked);
}

Seat.propTypes = {
    number:PropTypes.number,
    price:PropTypes.number,
    status:PropTypes.string
}

export default Seat;
```

Here, an important thing to note is that we are using JSX syntax, which we already saw in `chapter 2`, *Integrate React App with Firebase*.

Here, we have defined the `Seat` component with three properties:

- `number`: refers to the number or ID given to that seat
- `price`: refers to the amount to be charged to book this seat
- `status`: refers to the seat status if it is booked or available

`PropTypes` in React is used to validate the inputs your component receives; for example, the price should be a number and not a String. A warning will be shown in the JavaScript console if an invalid value is provided for a prop. For performance reasons, `PropTypes` checking will only take place in the development mode.

In our seat booking app, when a user selects a seat, we need to add it to the cart so that the user can check out/book the ticket(s). To do so, we need to handle an `onClick()` for a seat. For now, we are just printing a console statement in the click handler function, but we will need to write a logic to push the selected seats to the cart. We will look into it in the later section when we will integrate Redux in our app.

If any seat is already booked, obviously we won't allow the user to select it and hence based on the status, we are disabling seats if they are booked.

Seat is our basic building block, and it will receive data from the parent component, which is the `SeatRow` component.

`components/SeatRow.js`:

```javascript
import React from 'react'
import PropTypes from 'prop-types'
import Seat from './Seat';
const SeatRow = ({ seats, rowNumber }) => (
    <div>
        <li className="row">
            <ol className="seatrow">
                {seats.map(seat =>
                    <Seat key={seat.number} number={seat.number}
                        price={seat.price}
                        status={seat.status}
                    />
                )}
            </ol>
        </li>
    </div>
)
SeatRow.propTypes = {
    seats: PropTypes.arrayOf(PropTypes.shape({
        number: PropTypes.number,
```

```
      price: PropTypes.number,
      status: PropTypes.string
   }))
}
export default SeatRow;
```

A `SeatRow` represents a row of seats. We are creating loosely coupled components that can be maintained easily and can be reused wherever required. Here, we are iterating the array of seats JSON data to render corresponding `Seat` objects.

You can see in the preceding code block that we are validating our values using `PropTypes`. The `PropTypes.arrayOf` represents an array of Seats and `PropTypes.shape` represents the `Seat` object props.

Our next component is the `SeatList` component.

components/SeatList.js:

```
import React from 'react'
import PropTypes from 'prop-types'
const SeatList = ({ title, children }) => (

   <div>
      <h3>{title}</h3>
      <ol className="list">
         {children}
      </ol>
   </div>

)
SeatList.propTypes = {
children: PropTypes.node,
title: PropTypes.string.isRequired
}
export default SeatList;
```

Here, we have defined a `SeatList` component with two properties:

- `title`: A title to be displayed for seat booking
- `children`: It represents the list of Seats

There are two important things related to proptypes:

- `Proptypes.string.isRequired`: `isRequired` can be chained to ensure that you see a warning in the console if the data received is not valid.
- `Proptypes.node`: Node represents that anything can be rendered: number, string, elements, or an array (or fragment) containing these types.

The next and final component in our app is `Cart`.

`components/Cart.js`:

```
const Cart = () => {
  return (
    <div>
      <h3>No. of Seats selected: </h3>
      <button>
        Checkout
      </button>
    </div>
  )
}
export default Cart;
```

Our cart component will have a button called `Checkout` to book the tickets. It will also show the summary of the selected seats and total payment to be done. As of now, we are just putting a button and a label. We will modify it once we integrate Firebase and Redux in our app.

So, we have our presentational components ready. Now, let's integrate Firebase with our application.

Integrating Firebase Realtime Database

It's time to integrate Firebase in our application. Though we have already seen the detailed description and features of Firebase Realtime Database in Chapter 2, *Connecting React to Redux and Firebase,* we will see key concepts for JSON data architecture and best practices for the same. Firebase database stores data as a JSON tree.

Take into consideration this example:

```
{
  "seats" : {
    "seat-1" : {
```

```
         "number" : 1,
         "price" : 400,
         "rowNo" : 1,
         "status" : "booked"
      },
      "seat-2" : {
         "number" : 2,
         "price" : 400,
         "rowNo" : 1,
         "status" : "booked"
      },
      "seat-3" : {
         "number" : 3,
         "price" : 400,
         "rowNo" : 1,
         "status" : "booked"
      },
      "seat-4" : {
         "number" : 4,
         "price" : 400,
         "rowNo" : 1,
         "status" : "available"
      },
      ...
   }
}
```

The database uses a JSON tree, but data stored in the database can be represented as certain native types to help you write more maintainable code. As shown in the preceding example, we have created a tree structure like `seats > seat-#`. We are defining our own keys, such as `seat-1`, `seat-2`, and more, but if you use the `push` method, it will be autogenerated.

It is worth noting that Firebase Realtime Database data nesting can go up to 32 levels deep. However, it is recommended that you avoid the nesting as much as possible and have the flat data structure. If you have a flattened data structure, it provides you with two main benefits:

- Load/Fetch data that is needed: You will fetch only the required data and not a complete tree, because in the case of a nested tree if you load a node, you will load all the children of that node too.
- Security: You give limited access to data because in the case of a nested tree, if you give access to a parent node, it essentially means that you also grant access to the data under that node.

The best practices here are as listed:

- Avoid Nested Data
- Use Flatten data structures
- Create Scalable Data

Let's first create our Realtime Firebase database:

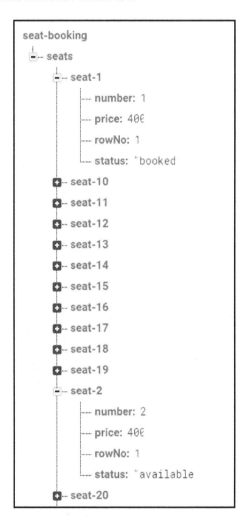

We can directly create this structure on Firebase console or create this JSON and import it in Firebase. We have the following structure to our data:

- Seats: Seats is our main node and contains a list of Seats
- Seat: Seat is an individual object that represents a seat with a unique number, price, and status

We can design a three-level deep nested data structure, such as `seats > row > seat`, for our sample application, but as mentioned in the best practices earlier, we should design a flattened data structure.

Now that we have our data designed, let's integrate the Firebase in our application. In this application, instead of adding Fireabase dependency through URL, we will add its module using `npm`:

```
npm install firebase
```

This command will install Firebase module in our application, and we can import it using the following statement:

```
import firebase from 'firebase';
```

The import statement is ES6 feature, so if you are not aware of it, refer to ES6 documentation at `http://es6-features.org/`.

We will put our DB related files in a folder called API.

`api/firebase.js`:

```
import firebase from 'firebase'
var config = { /* COPY THE ACTUAL CONFIG FROM FIREBASE CONSOLE */
apiKey:"AIzaSyBkdkAcHdNpOEP_W9NnOxpQy4m1deMbG5Vooo",
authDomain:"seat-booking.firebaseapp.com",
databaseURL:"https://seat-booking.firebaseio.com",
projectId:"seat-booking",
storageBucket:"seat-booking.appspot.com",
messagingSenderId:"248063178000"
};
var fire = firebase.initializeApp(config);
export default fire;
```

The preceding code will initialize the Firebase instance that can be used to connect to Firebase. For better separation of concern, we will also create a file called `service.js`, which will interact with our database.

`api/service.js`:

```
import fire from './firebase.js';

export function getSeats() {
    let seatArr = [];
    let rowArray = [];
    const noOfSeatsInARow = 5;

    return new Promise((resolve, reject) => {
        //iterate through seat array and create row wise groups/array
        const seatsRef =
fire.database().ref('seats/').orderByChild("number");
        seatsRef.once('value', function (snapshot) {
            snapshot.forEach(function (childSnapshot) {
                var childData = childSnapshot.val();
                seatArr.push({
                    number: childData.number,
                    price: childData.price,
                    status: childData.status,
                    rowNo: childData.rowNo
                });
            });

            var groups = [], i;
            for (i = 0; i < seatArr.length; i += noOfSeatsInARow) {
                groups = seatArr.slice(i, i + noOfSeatsInARow);
                console.log(groups);
                rowArray.push({
                    id: i,
                    seats: groups
                })
            }
            console.log(rowArray);
            resolve(rowArray);
        }).catch(error => { reject(error) });
    })

}

export function bookSelSeats(seats) {
    console.log("book seats", seats);
    return new Promise((resolve, reject) => {
```

```
        //write logic for payment
        seats.forEach(obj => {
            fire.database().ref('seats/').child("seat-" + obj.number)
                .update({ status: "booked"
}).then(resolve(true)).catch(error => { reject(error) });
        })
    });


}
```

In this file, we have mainly defined two functions—getSeats() and bookSelSeats()—which are to read database for list of seats and update seats when user checks them out from the cart, respectively.

Firebase provides two methods—on() and once()—to read data at a path and listen for changes. There is a difference between the on and once methods:

1. The on method: It will listen for the data changes and will receive the data at the specified location in the database at the time of the event. Also, it doesn't return a Promise object.
2. The once method: It will be called only once and will not listen for changes. It will return a Promise object.

As we are using the once method, we get a Promise object returned to our component object, since the call from our component to the service will be async. You will understand it better in the following App.js file.

To read a static snapshot of the contents at a given path, we can use value event. This method is executed once when the listener is attached and every time the data changes including children. The event callback is passed a snapshot containing all data at that location, including child data. If there is no data, the snapshot returned is null.

 It is important to note that the value event will be fired every time the data is changed at the given path, including data changes in children. Hence, it is recommended that we attach the listener only at the lowest level needed to limit the snapshot size.

Here, we are getting the data from Firebase Realtime Database and get all the seats. Once we get the data, we create a JSON object according to the format we need and return it.

App.js will be our container component and will look like the one that follows:

App.js

```
import React, { Component } from 'react';
import './App.css';
import SeatList from './components/SeatList';
import Cart from './components/Cart';
import { getSeats } from './api/service.js';
import SeatRow from './components/SeatRow';

class App extends Component {
  constructor() {
    super();
    this.state = {
      seatrows: [],
    }
  }

  componentDidMount() {
    let _this = this;
    getSeats().then(function (list) {
      console.log(list);
      _this.setState({
        seatrows: list,
      });
    });

  }

  render() {
    return (
      <div className="layout">
        <SeatList title="Seats">
          {this.state.seatrows.map((row, index) =>
            <SeatRow
              seats={row.seats}
              key={index}
            />
          )}

        </SeatList>
        <hr />
        <Cart />
      </div>
    )
```

```
    }
  }

export default App;
```

Here, we can see that the `App` component maintains the state. However, our goal is to separate the state management from our presentational component and use Redux for it.

So, now we have all functional pieces ready, but how will it look without proper design and CSS. We have to design a seat layout that is user-friendly, so let's apply CSS. We have a file called `App.css` for the entire app. We can separate them out in different files if required.

App.css:

```
.layout {
  margin: 19px auto;
  max-width: 350px;
}
*, *:before, *:after {
  box-sizing: border-box;
}
.list {
  border-right: 4px solid grey;
  border-left: 4px solid grey;
}

html {
  font-size: 15px;
}

ol {
  list-style: none;
  padding: 0;
  margin: 0;
}

.seatrow {
  display: flex;
  flex-direction: row;
  flex-wrap: nowrap;
  justify-content: flex-start;
}
.seatobj {
  display: flex;
  flex: 0 0 17.28571%;
  padding: 5px;
  position: relative;
```

```
  }

.seatobj label {
  display: block;
  position: relative;
  width: 100%;
  text-align: center;
  font-size: 13px;
  font-weight: bold;
  line-height: 1.4rem;
  padding: 4px 0;
  background:#bada60;
  border-radius: 4px;
  animation-duration: 350ms;
  animation-fill-mode: both;
}

.seatobj:nth-child(2) {
  margin-right: 14.28571%;
}
.seatobj input[type=checkbox] {
  position: absolute;
  opacity: 0;
}
.seatobj input[type=checkbox]:checked + label {
  background: #f42530;
}

.seatobj input[type=checkbox]:disabled + label:after {
  content: "X";
  text-indent: 0;
  position: absolute;
  top: 4px;
  left: 49%;
  transform: translate(-49%, 0%);
}
.seatobj input[type=checkbox]:disabled + label:hover {
  box-shadow: none;
  cursor: not-allowed;
}

.seatobj label:before {
  content: "";
  position: absolute;
  width: 74%;
  height: 74%;
  top: 1px;
  left: 49%;
```

```
  transform: translate(-49%, 0%);
  border-radius: 2px;
}
.seatobj label:hover {
  cursor: pointer;
  box-shadow: 0 0 0px 3px yellowgreen;
}
.seatobj input[type=checkbox]:disabled + label {
  background: #dde;
  text-indent: -9999px;
  overflow: hidden;
}
```

We are done with our minimal seat booking app. Yay! The following are the screenshots of the application.

The next screenshot shows the default layout where all the seats are available for booking:

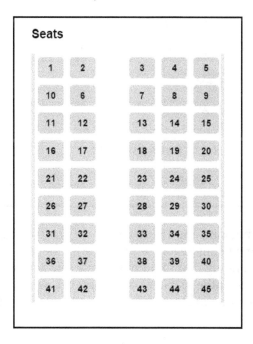

The following screenshot shows that the Booked tickets are marked as **X**, so the user can't select them. It also shows that when a user selects a seat, it turns out to be red so that they can know which seats have been selected by them:

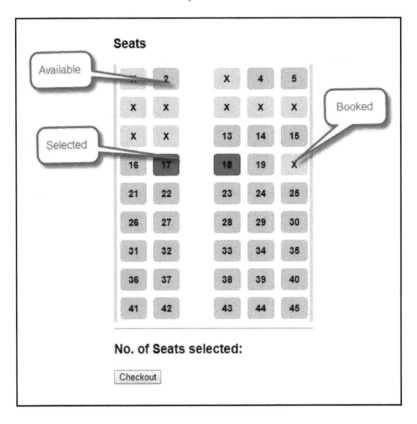

Finally, we have our seat booking app ready where we are loading data from Firebase database and showing them using React. However, after looking at the preceding screenshot, you must be thinking that though we have selected two seats, the cart is empty and is not showing any data of the seats. If you remember, we haven't written any logic in the seat click handler function to add the selected seats in cart and hence our cart remains empty.

So, now the question would be, since Seat and Cart components are not directly related to each other, how will a Seat component communicate with the Cart component? Let's find an answer to this question.

When components are not related or are related but too far away in the hierarchy, we can use an external event system to notify anyone who wants to listen.

Redux is a popular choice to handle the data and events in a React application. It's a *simplified* version of the Flux pattern. Let's explore Redux in detail.

What is Redux?

In this technological era, since the requirements for web applications have become increasingly complicated, the state management of an application has a lot of challenges at the code level. For example, in Realtime applications, a lot of data is stored in the cache for faster retrieval apart from the data that is persisted in the database. Similarly, on the UI side, due to complex User Interfaces such as multiple tabs, multiple routes, pagination, filters, and breadcrumbs and more, application state management becomes a very difficult task.

In any application, different components exist, which interact with each other to produce a particular output or a state. There will also be chances that this interaction is so complex that you lost control over the application state. For example, a component or a model updating another component or a model that in turn causes an update of another view. This type of code is difficult to manage. It becomes challenging to add a new feature or fix any bugs because you don't know when a small change will affect another working functionality.

To reduce such issues, libraries like React removed the direct DOM manipulation and also asynchrony. However, it is only applied to view or presentation layer. The state management of your data is up to the application developers. This is where Redux comes into the picture.

Redux is a framework that manages states in a JavaScript app. This is what the official site says:

Redux is a predictable state container for JavaScript apps.

Redux attempts to make state mutations predictable by imposing certain restrictions on how and when updates can happen. We will see what these restrictions are and how they work shortly, but before that, let's understand the core concept of Redux.

Redux is very simple. When we talk about Redux, we need to remember three core terms: Store, Action, and Reducer. Here's what they are:

1. **Store**: The state of your application will be managed by Store, which is an object that maintains the application's state tree. Remember that there should be a single Store in your Redux app. Also, due to imposed restrictions, you can't directly manipulate or mutate the application store.

2. **Action**: To change something in your store, you need to dispatch an Action. An action is nothing but a plain JavaScript object that describes what has happened. Actions allow us to understand what is happening in the app and why and hence makes the state predictable.

3. **Reducer**: Finally, to glue actions and state together, we write a Reducer, which is a simple JavaScript function that takes state and action as arguments and returns the new state of the app.

Since we now have a basic understanding of Redux, let's check the three fundamental principles of Redux, which are as listed:

1. **Single source of truth**: A store is simply a state container. As mentioned, in your React App, there should be only a single store and hence it is considered as source of Truth. A single object tree also makes it easy to debug the app.

2. **State is Read Only**: To change the state, application has to emit an Action that describes what has happened. No views or other functions can directly write to the state. This restriction prevents any unwanted state changes. Each action will be performed on a centralized object and in order so that we can get an up-to-date state at any point of time. As actions are just plain objects, we can debug and serialize them for testing purposes.

3. **Changes are made with Pure Functions**: To describe transformation of the state tree by dispatched actions, write Pure Functions/Reducers. What does the term Pure Function mean? A function is pure if it returns the same value every time a given set of arguments is passed to it. Pure functions do not modify their input arguments. Instead, they use the input to calculate a value and then return that calculated value. Our reducers are pure functions that take state and action as inputs and return new state and not the mutated state. You can have as many reducers as you want, and it is also recommended that you split big reducers to smaller reducers that can manage a specific part of your application tree. Reducers are JavaScript functions, so you can pass additional data to them. They can be built like common functions, which can be used across the application of Presentational and Container components.

Presentational and Container components

In our application, Seat List is responsible of fetching the data and rendering it. This is okay and works well for small or sample applications, but with this, we lose a few benefits of React, one of which is reusability. `SeatList` can't be reused easily unless under the exact same circumstances, so what's the solution?

We know that this kind of issue is common across different programming languages, and we have solutions in terms of Design Patterns. Similarly, the solution to our problem is a pattern called **Container Component pattern**.

So, instead of our React component, out Container component will take the responsibility of fetching the data and passing it to the corresponding subcomponent. In simple terms, a container fetches the data and then renders its subcomponent.

React bindings for Redux has also accepted the idea of separation of **Presentational and Container components.** Presentational Components are concerned about how things will look to the user rather than being concerned about how things will work. Similarly, Container components are concerned about how things work rather than how things look.

Let's look at the comparison in this table:

Presentational Components	Container Components
Concerned about the user view or how things will look	Concerned about the data and how things will work
Get/read data from parent components as props	Are connected to Redux State
Have DOM markup and styles on their own	Very less or no DOM markup and no styles on their own
Rarely Stateful	Are often Stateful
Handwritten	Can be handwritten or generated by React Redux

As we now know the difference between Presentational and Container Components, we should know the benefits of this separation of concerns:

- Reusability of components
- Can reduce the duplicate code and have more manageable applications
- Different teams, such as Designers and JS/Application developers can work parallelly

Before we start integrating Redux into our app, let's go through the basic building blocks and API of Redux.

Basics of Redux

Redux is quite simple, so don't be afraid by just looking at the fancy terms such as Reducers, Actions, and such. We will go through the basic building blocks of Redux application, and you will also feel the same.

Actions

As we saw at the beginning of the chapter, an action is nothing but a plain JavaScript object that describes what has happened. To change the state is to emit an action that describes what has happened. Also, for store, actions are only the source of truth or information.

Here's an example action creator.

Each action type should be defined as a constant:

```
const fetchSeats = rows => ({
    type: GET_SEATS,
    rows
})
```

The `type` of an action describes the kind of the action that has occurred. If your application is large enough, you may separate out the action types as string constants to a separate module/file and use it in actions.

Now, you might be having a question—what should be the structure of my action ? We have here type and then have directly added rows. The answer to your question is that except the type, you can have any structure of your action. However, there is a standard for defining an action.

An action must be a JavaScript Object and must have a type property. Also, an action may have an error or payload property. The payload property can be any type of value. In the preceding example, `rows` represent a payload.

Action creators

Action creators are functions that create actions; for example, `function fetchSeats(){return{type:FETCH_SEATS,rows}}`.

Actions often trigger a dispatch when invoked, for example, `dispatch(fetchSeats(seats)).`

Note that action creators can also be asynchronous and hence we need to handle async flow in our logic. It is an advanced topic and can be referred to on the Redux website.

Reducers

Actions only specify what has happened but do not specify what is the effect of that action on the application state. The reducer function specifies how the application state is changed. It is a pure function that takes the two arguments—previous state and an action—and returns the next updated state.

```
(previousState, action) =>newState
```

Things you should **never** do inside a reducer:

- Modify its arguments
- API calls and routing
- Call other non-pure functions, for example, `Date.now()`

In Redux, a single object represents the application state. So, before we write any code, it is very important to think and decide the structure of the application state object.

It is recommended that we keep our state object as normalized as possible and avoid nesting of objects.

Store

As described initially, the store is the main object that holds the application state tree. It's important to note that there will be a single store in a Redux application. When there is a requirement of splitting the data handling logic, you'll use the Reducer Composition pattern instead of creating many stores.

The following methods are available for Store:

- `getState()`: Gives the current state tree of the application
- `dispatch(action)`: Used to dispatch an action
- `subscribe(listener)`: Subscribe to the store changes
- `replaceReducer(nextReducer)`: It is an advanced API that replaces the currently used Reducer by Store

Data flow

We have seen the core components of the Redux architecture. Now, let's understand how all these components actually work together. Redux architecture supports only single directional data flow, as illustrated in the following diagram. This means that all the data in an application passes through the defined workflow in a single direction, which makes the logic of your application more easy.

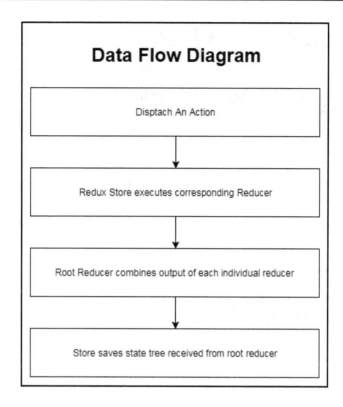

Advanced topics in Redux

Once you are through the basics, there are some advanced topics to go through, such as **React Router**, **Ajax and Async Actions**, and **Middleware**. We will not cover them here since they are out of the scope of this book. However, we will just look at the important topic of Middleware in brief.

By default, Redux supports synchronous data flow only. To have asynchronous data flow, you will need to use Middleware. Middleware is nothing but a framework or library that provides a wrapper for your dispatch method and allows to pass functions and promises rather than just actions. Middleware is being used to mainly support asynchronous actions. There are many middlewares out there, such as redux-thunk for asynchronous actions. Middlewares are also useful for logging or crash reporting. We will also use redux-thunk in our application. To enhance `createStore()`, we need to use the `applyMiddleware(...middleware)` function.

Seat booking with Redux

Let's enhance our seat booking app by integrating the Redux.

We can install React Bindings explicitly, using the following command, since they are not included in Redux by default:

```
npm install --save react-redux
```

Now, we will extend our seat booking app by integrating Redux. There will be a lot of changes as it will impact all of our components. Here, we will start with our entry point.

src/index.js:

```
import React from 'react'
import { render } from 'react-dom'
import { createStore, applyMiddleware } from 'redux'
import SeatBookingApp from './containers/SeatBookingApp'
import { Provider } from 'react-redux'
import { createLogger } from 'redux-logger'
import thunk from 'redux-thunk'
import reducer from './reducers'
import { getAllSeats } from './actions'


const middleware = [thunk];
//middleware will print the logs for state changes
if (process.env.NODE_ENV !== 'production') {
    middleware.push(createLogger());
}

const store = createStore(
    reducer,
    applyMiddleware(...middleware)
)

store.dispatch(getAllSeats())

render(
    <Provider store={store}>
        <SeatBookingApp />
    </Provider>,
    document.getElementById('root')
)
```

Let's understand our code:

- `<Provide store>`: Makes the Redux Store available to the component hierarchy. Note that you cannot use `connect()` without wrapping a parent component in a provider.
- `<SeatBookingApp>`: It is our parent component and will be defined under Container components package. It will have code similar to what we have in `App.js`, which we saw earlier.
- `Middleware`: It is like an interceptor in other languages that provides a third-party extension point between dispatching an action and the moment it reaches the reducer, for example, Logging or Logger. If you don't apply a middleware, you would need to add loggers manually in all the actions and reducers.
- `applyMiddleware`: It tells Redux store how to handle and set up the middleware. Note the usage of a rest parameter (...middleware); it denotes that the `applyMiddleware` function accepts multiple arguments (any number) and can get them as an array. A key feature of Middleware is that multiple middleware can be combined together.

We will also need to change our presentational components little bit as per Redux state management.

Let's start with Cart component.

`components/Cart.js`:

```
import React from 'react'
import PropTypes from 'prop-types'
const Cart = ({seats,total, onCheckoutClicked}) => {
  const hasSeats = seats.length > 0
  const nodes = hasSeats ? (
    seats.map(seat =>
      <div>
        Seat Number: {seat.number} - Price: {seat.price}
      </div>
    )
  ) : (
    <em>No seats selected</em>
  )

  return (
    <div>
    <b>Selected Seats</b> <br/>
      {nodes} <br/>
    <b>Total</b> <br/>
```

```
        {total}
        <br/>
        <button onClick={onCheckoutClicked}>
          Checkout
        </button>
      </div>
    )
  }

  Cart.propTypes = {
    seats: PropTypes.array,
    total: PropTypes.string,
    onCheckoutClicked: PropTypes.func
  }
  export default Cart;
```

Our cart component receives a checkout function from the parent component that will dispatch checkout action along with seats, which are added in cart.

`components/Seat.js`:

```
  import React from 'react'
  import PropTypes from 'prop-types'

  const Seat = ({ number, price, status, rowNo, handleClick }) => {
    return (

      <li className={'seatobj ' + status} key={number.toString()}>
        <input type="checkbox" disabled={status === "booked" ? true : false}
  id={number.toString()} onClick={handleClick} />
        <label htmlFor={number.toString()}>{number}</label>
      </li>

    )
  }

  Seat.propTypes = {
    number: PropTypes.number,
    price: PropTypes.number,
    status: PropTypes.string,
    rowNo: PropTypes.number,
    handleClick: PropTypes.func
  }

  export default Seat;
```

Our Seat component receives its state from the parent component along with the `handleClick` function that dispatches the `ADD_TO_CART` action.

components/SeatList.js:

```
import React from 'react'
import PropTypes from 'prop-types'

const SeatList = ({ title, children }) => (

  <div>
    <h3>{title}</h3>
    <ol className="list">
      {children}
    </ol>
  </div>
)

SeatList.propTypes = {
  children: PropTypes.node,
  title: PropTypes.string.isRequired
}

export default SeatList;
```

`SeatList` receives seats data from the container component.

components/SeatRow.js:

```
import React from 'react'
import PropTypes from 'prop-types'
import Seat from './Seat';

const SeatRow = ({ seats, rowNumber, onAddToCartClicked }) => {
  return (
  <div>
    <li className="row row--1" key="1">
      <ol className="seatrow">
        {seats.map(seat =>
          <Seat key={seat.number} number={seat.number}
            price={seat.price}
            status={seat.status}
            rowNo={seat.rowNo}
            handleClick={() => onAddToCartClicked(seat)}
          />
        )}
```

```
        </ol>
      </li>
    </div>
  )
  }
  SeatRow.propTypes = {
    seats: PropTypes.arrayOf(PropTypes.shape({
      number: PropTypes.number,
      price: PropTypes.number,
      status: PropTypes.string,
      rowNo: PropTypes.number
    })),
    rowNumber: PropTypes.number,
    onAddToCartClicked: PropTypes.func.isRequired
  }

  export default SeatRow;
```

`SeatRow` receives all seats for that particular row.

Let's check our container components.

`containers/SeatBookingApp.js`:

```
  import React from 'react'
  import SeatContainer from './SeatContainer'
  import CartContainer from './SeatCartContainer'
  import '../App.css';

  const SeatBookingApp = () => (
      <div className="layout">
          <h2>Ticket Booking App</h2>
          <hr />
          <SeatContainer />
          <hr />
          <CartContainer />
      </div>
  )
  export default SeatBookingApp;
```

It is our parent component and includes the other child container components:
`SeatContainer` and `CartContainer`.

`container/SeatCartContainer.js`:

```
  import React from 'react'
  import PropTypes from 'prop-types'
```

```
import { connect } from 'react-redux'
import { bookSeats } from '../actions'
import { getTotal, getCartSeats } from '../reducers'
import Cart from '../components/Cart'

const CartContainer = ({ seats, total, bookSeats }) => {

    return (

    <Cart
        seats={seats}
        total={total}
        onCheckoutClicked={() => bookSeats(seats)}
    />
)
}
CartContainer.propTypes = {
    seats: PropTypes.arrayOf(PropTypes.shape({
        number: PropTypes.number.isRequired,
        rowNo: PropTypes.number.isRequired,
        price: PropTypes.number.isRequired,
        status: PropTypes.string.isRequired
    })).isRequired,
    total: PropTypes.string,
    bookSeats: PropTypes.func.isRequired
}
const mapStateToProps = (state) => ({
    seats: getCartSeats(state),
    total: getTotal(state)
})

export default connect(mapStateToProps, {bookSeats})(CartContainer)
```

This container component will be interacting with the store and will pass data to child component—Cart.

Let's understand the code:

1. mapStateToProps: It is a function that will be called each time the Store is updated which means component is subscribed to store updates.
2. {bookSeats}: It can be a function or an object that Redux provides so that container can easily pass that function to the child component on its props. We are passing the bookSeats function so that the Checkout button in the Cart component can call it.
3. connect(): Connects a React component to a Redux store.

Let's see our next container—`SeatContainer`.

`containers/SeatContainer.js`:

```
import React from 'react'
import PropTypes from 'prop-types'
import { connect } from 'react-redux'
import { addSeatToCart } from '../actions'
import SeatRow from '../components/SeatRow'
import SeatList from '../components/SeatList'
import { getAllSeats } from '../reducers/seats';

const SeatContainer = ({ seatrows, addSeatToCart }) => {
    return (
    <SeatList title="Seats">
        {seatrows.map((row, index) =>
            <SeatRow key={index}
                seats={row.seats}
                rowNumber={index}
                onAddToCartClicked={addSeatToCart} />

        )}

    </SeatList>

)
}
SeatContainer.propTypes = {
    seatrows: PropTypes.arrayOf(PropTypes.shape({
        number: PropTypes.number,
        price: PropTypes.number,
        status: PropTypes.string,
        rowNo: PropTypes.number
    })).isRequired,
    addSeatToCart: PropTypes.func.isRequired
}

const mapStateToProps = state => ({
    seatrows: getAllSeats(state.seats)
})

export default connect(mapStateToProps,  { addSeatToCart })(SeatContainer)
```

As explained earlier for `CartContainer`, we will have a similar code structure for `SeatContainer`.

Now, we will create a `constants` file that defines the constants for our `Actions`. Though you can directly define constants in the file where you have your action, it is a good practice to define the constants in a separate file as it is much easier to maintain the clean code.

`constants/ActionTypeConstants.js`:

```
//get the list of seats
export const GET_SEATS = 'GET_SEATS'
//add seats to cart on selection
export const ADD_TO_CART = 'ADD_TO_CART'
//book seats
export const CHECKOUT = 'CHECKOUT'
```

We will have three actions:

- `GET_SEATS`: To fetch the seats data from Firebase and populate on UI
- `ADD_TO_CART`: To add the selected seats in user cart
- `CHECKOUT`: Book the seats

Let's define the actions in a file called `index.js`.

`actions/index.js`:

```
import { getSeats,bookSelSeats } from '../api/service';
import { GET_SEATS, ADD_TO_CART, CHECKOUT } from
'../constants/ActionTypeConstants';

//action creator for getting seats
const fetchSeats = rows => ({
    type: GET_SEATS,
    rows
})

//action getAllSeats
export const getAllSeats = () => dispatch => {
    getSeats().then(function (rows) {
        dispatch(fetchSeats(rows));
    });
}

//action creator for add seat to cart
const addToCart = seat => ({
    type: ADD_TO_CART,
    seat
})
```

```
export const addSeatToCart = seat => (dispatch, getState) => {
    dispatch(addToCart(seat))

}

export const bookSeats = seats => (dispatch, getState) => {
    const { cart } = getState()
    bookSelSeats(seats).then(function() {
        dispatch({
            type: CHECKOUT,
            cart
        })
    });
}
```

Actions send data from your application to your store using the dispatcher() method. Here, we have two functions:

- fetchSeats(): It is action creator, which creates the GET_SEATS action
- getAllSeats(): It is actual action that dispatches data to store, which we get by calling the getSeats() method of our service

Likewise, we can define our actions for the rest of the two actions: ADD_TO_CART and CHECKOUT.

Now, let's see the reducers. We will start with seats reducer.

reducers/seats.js:

```
import { GET_SEATS } from "../constants/ActionTypeConstants";
import { combineReducers } from 'redux'

const seatRow = (state = {}, action) => {
    switch (action.type) {
        case GET_SEATS:
            return {
                ...state,
                ...action.rows.reduce((obj, row) => {
                    obj[row.id] = row
                    return obj
                }, {})
            }
        default:
            return state
    }
}
```

```
const rowIds = (state = [], action) => {
    switch (action.type) {
        case GET_SEATS:
            return action.rows.map(row => row.id)
        default:
            return state
    }
}

export default combineReducers({
    seatRow,
    rowIds
})

export const getRow = (state, number) =>
    state.seatRow[number]



export const getAllSeats = state =>
    state.rowIds.map(number => getRow(state, number))
```

Let's understand this piece of code:

- `combineReducers`: We have split our Reducer into different functions—`rowIds` and `seatRow`—and defined the root reducer as a function that calls the reducers managing different parts of the state and combines them into a single object

Similarly, we will have cart reducer.

`reducers/cart.js`:

```
import {
    ADD_TO_CART,
    CHECKOUT
} from '../constants/ActionTypeConstants'

const initialState = {
    addedSeats: []
}

const addedSeats = (state = initialState.addedSeats, action) => {
    switch (action.type) {
        case ADD_TO_CART:
        //if it is already there, remove it from cart
        if (state.indexOf(action.seat) !== -1) {
            return state.filter(seatobj=>seatobj!=action.seat);
```

```
        }
        return [...state, action.seat]
        default:
            return state
    }
}

export const getAddedSeats = state => state.addedSeats

const cart = (state = initialState, action) => {
    switch (action.type) {
        case CHECKOUT:
            return initialState
        default:
            return {
                addedSeats: addedSeats(state.addedSeats, action)
            }
    }
}

export default cart
```

It exposes reducer functions related to cart operations.

Now, we will have a final combine reducer.

`reducers/index.js`:

```
import { combineReducers } from 'redux'
import seats from './seats'
import cart, * as cartFunc from './cart'

export default combineReducers({
    cart,
    seats
})

const getAddedSeats = state => cartFunc.getAddedSeats(state.cart)

export const getTotal = state =>
    getAddedSeats(state)
        .reduce((total, seat) =>
            total + seat.price,
        0
        )
        .toFixed(2)

export const getCartSeats = state =>
```

```
getAddedSeats(state).map(seat => ({
    ...seat
}))
```

It is a `combineReducers` for seats and cart. It also exposes some common function to calculate total in cart and to get the seats added in cart. That's it. We have finally introduced Redux to manage our state of the application, and we have our seat booking app ready using React, Redux, and Firebase.

Summary

In this chapter, we explored React and Firebase in depth. We talked about the structure of the data in Firebase database and have seen that we should avoid data nesting as much as possible. We have also seen the usage of the `on` and `once` methods with respect to data reading and also the event called 'value', which gets fired when data changes in your database. We also went through the core concepts of Redux and saw how easy it is to use Redux for the state management of the application. We also looked at the difference between Presentational and Container components and how they should be designed. Then, we talked about the basics of Redux and also talked briefly about the advanced topics of Redux.

Moreover, we created a seat booking application with the usage of all three—React, Redux and Firebase—and saw a real-life practical example of the smooth integration of all them.

In the next chapter, we will explore Firebase Admin SDK and see how to implement User and Access Management.

5
User Profile and Access Management

In the last chapter, we saw how we can use the Firebase with the react-redux application. We also explored Redux in detail and saw how and when we need to use Redux in our React app, and Firebase Realtime Database will give us the Realtime seat booking status in our application. In this chapter, we will go through Firebase Admin SDK, which provides a user management API to read and write Realtime Database data with full admin privileges. So we will create an admin page for our application where we have the ability to perform the actions such as the following:

- Creating new users
- User search engine where we can search the users by different criteria
- List of all the users
- Accessing the user metadata, which includes the account creation date and last sign-in date for the particular user
- Deleting the users
- Updating the user information without having to sign in as the user
- Verifying emails
- Changing a user's email without sending an email notification to revoke these changes
- Creating a new user with a phone number and changing the user's phone number without sending SMS verification

First, we need to do the setup of Firebase Admin SDK in Node.js environment to perform the preceding actions as an admin.

Setting up Firebase Admin SDK

For using Firebase Admin SDK, we'll need a Firebase project where we have service account to communicate with the Firebase services and a configuration file that includes the service account's credentials.

To configure the Firebase Admin SDK, follow these steps:

1. Log in to `Firebase Console`, select the `<project_name>` project, and click on the setting icon in **Project Overview**:

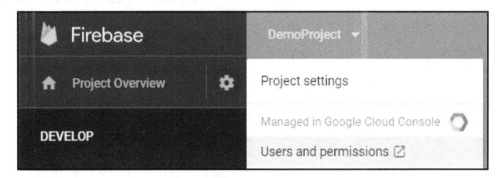

Overview tab

2. Go to the **Service Accounts** tab inside **Project Settings**.

3. Click on the **GENERATE PRIVATE KEY** button at the bottom of Firebase admin section; it will generate the JSON file that contains the service account credentials:

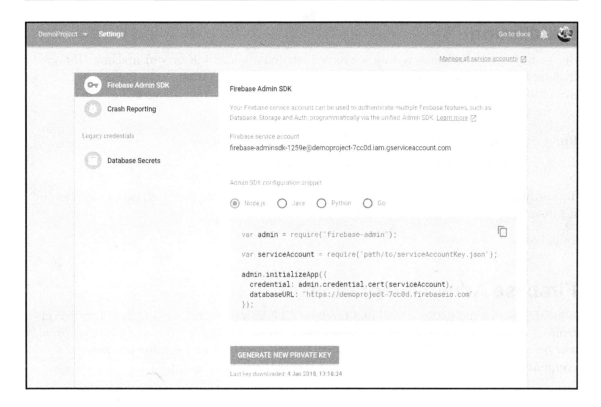

This JSON file contains very sensitive information about your service account and private encryption key. So never share and store it in a public repository; keep it confidential. If we lose this file because of any reason then, we can generate it again, and we'll no longer access Firebase Admin SDK with the old file.

Firebase CLI

Firebase provides a command-line interface, which provides a variety of tools to create, manage, view, and deploy Firebase projects. Using Firebase CLI, we can easily deploy and host our application on production grade static hosting, and it is automatically served by HTTPS and backed by global CDN in one single command.

Installation

Before the installation, ensure that we have installed Node.js 4.0+ on our machine. If not installed, then download the latest version of Node.js 8 "LTS" from `https://nodejs.org` Once we're done with the installation, we can download the Firebase CLI from `npm` (node package manager).

Run this command to install Firebase CLI globally on your system:

```
npm install -g firebase-tools
```

To verify the installation, run the following command; it prints the Firebase CLI version if it's installed properly on your system:

```
firebase --version
```

Firebase Admin Integration

Now that we've successfully installed Firebase CLI, let's copy the existing application code from `Chapter 3`, *Authentication with Firebase*, to the new directory in `Chapter 5`, *User Profile and Access Management*. Here, we'll initialize the Firebase app and run the following command to log in to the Firebase console before initializing the app:

```
firebase login
```

Once you are successfully logged in to the Firebase console, run the following command to initialize the project:

```
firebase init
```

Once we run this command, it will prompt you to select the Firebase feature, project, and directory folder (relative to your project directory) that will contain `hosting` assets to be uploaded with the `firebase deploy` command (by default, it is public).

```
You can create multiple project aliases by running firebase use --add,
but for now we'll just set up a default project.

? Select a default Firebase project for this directory: DemoProject (demoproject-7cc0d)

=== Database Setup

Firebase Realtime Database Rules allow you to define how your data should be
structured and when your data can be read from and written to.

? What file should be used for Database Rules? database.rules.json
+ Database Rules for demoproject-7cc0d have been downloaded to database.rules.json.
Future modifications to database.rules.json will update Database Rules when you run
firebase deploy.

=== Hosting Setup

Your public directory is the folder (relative to your project directory) that
will contain Hosting assets to be uploaded with firebase deploy. If you
have a build process for your assets, use your build's output directory.

? What do you want to use as your public directory? build
? Configure as a single-page app (rewrite all urls to /index.html)? Yes
? File build/index.html already exists. Overwrite? No
i  Skipping write of build/index.html

i  Writing configuration info to firebase.json...
i  Writing project information to .firebaserc...

+ Firebase initialization complete!
```

We can also add features later on in our project, and it's also possible to associate multiple projects with the same directory.

Once Firebase initialization is complete, run the following command to install the project dependencies and then build the project:

```
//run this command to install the project dependencies
npm install

//run this command to build the project
npm run build
```

To run our application locally to verify before deploying to the production, run the following command:

```
firebase serve
```

It will start the server locally from build directory or whatever the name you have defined in the `firebase.json` file:

Name	Date modified	Type	Size
build	29-01-2018 15:49	File folder	
node_modules	26-01-2018 19:07	File folder	
public	23-01-2018 14:40	File folder	
src	31-01-2018 02:48	File folder	
.firebaserc	21-01-2018 03:24	FIREBASERC File	1 KB
.gitignore	09-12-2017 01:49	GITIGNORE File	1 KB
database.rules.json	21-01-2018 03:23	JSON File	1 KB
firebase.json	21-01-2018 03:24	JSON File	1 KB
package.json	29-01-2018 15:03	JSON File	1 KB
package-lock.json	26-01-2018 18:54	JSON File	387 KB
README.md	09-12-2017 01:49	MD File	107 KB

This is what our folder structure looks like after firebase initialization using the firebase CLI.

Using the Firebase Admin Auth API with React

The Firebase Admin SDK will give us the power to integrate your own server using the Firebase Auth API. With Firebase Admin SDK, we can manage our application users such as `View`, `Create`, `Update`, and `Delete` without requiring a user's credentials or manage authentication tokens without going to Firebase Admin Console.

To implement this, we will create Admin Panel in our existing React application.

Here's the list of features we'll integrate into our Admin Panel using Firebase Admin SDK:

- Create and verify the custom token
- User Level Access Roles with Custom user claims
- View list of app users
- Fetch user profile
- `Create`, `Delete`, and `Update` the user information
- Resolve the Ticket status

Initializing the Admin SDK

As we saw, Firebase admin SDK is only supported in Node.Js, so we'll create a new project with npm init and install the firebase admin from the `npm` package.

Run the following command to install firebase admin and save it in your `package.json`:

```
npm install firebase-admin --save
```

Copy the following snippet in your JS file and initialize the SDK; we have added the reference to the JSON file that we downloaded from the Firebase Admin Service account:

```
const admin = require('firebase-admin');
const serviceAccount = require('./firebase/serviceAccountKey.json');

admin.initializeApp({
    credential: admin.credential.cert(serviceAccount),
    databaseURL: "https://demoproject-7cc0d.firebaseio.com"
});
```

Now we'll just create Restful API to interact with client App to access Admin SDK features.

Run this command to start the node admin server:

```
node <fileName>
```

It will start the local server on a different port, such as `http://localhost:3001`.

Creating and verifying custom token

The Firebase Admin SDK provides us an ability to authenticate the user with an external mechanism such as LDAP server, or third-party OAuth provider, which Firebase doesn't support, such as Instagram or LinkedIn. We can do all these things with Firebase custom tokens method, which is built-in Admin SDK, or we can use any third-party JWT libraries.

Let's see how we can create and validate token with Admin SDK.

For creating a custom token, we must have a valid `uid`, which we need to pass in the `createCustomToken()` method:

```
function createCustomToken(req,res){
 const userId = req.body.uid "guest_user"
 admin.auth().createCustomToken(userId)
 .then(function(customToken) {
```

```
    res.send(customToken.toJSON());
    })
    .catch(function(error) {
    console.log("Error creating custom token:", error);
    });
    }
```

In the preceding function, we have `uid` from client side when the user signs in with username and password, and if the credentials are valid, we'll return custom JWT (JSON Web Token) from the server that can be used by a client device to authenticate with Firebase:

```
app.get('/login', function (req, res) {
  if(validCredentials(req.body.username, req.body.password)){
      createCustomToken(req, res);
  }
})
```

Once it's authenticated, this identity will be used for accessing Firebase services like Firebase Realtime Database and Cloud Storage.

If need be, we can also add some additional fields to be included in the custom token. Consider this code:

```
function createCustomToken(req, res){
 const userId = req.body.uid
 const subscription = {
   paid:true
 }
 admin.auth().createCustomToken(userId)
 .then(function(customToken) {
   res.send(customToken.toJSON());
 })
 .catch(function(error) {
 console.log("Error creating custom token:", error);
 });
 }
```

These additional fields will be available in the `auth/request.auth` object in security rules.

Once the token is generated and received by the react method, we'll authenticate the user to the app by passing the custom token to the Firebase `signInWithCustomToken()` method:

```
const uid = this.state.userId
fetch('http://localhost:3000/login', {
    method: 'POST', // or 'PUT'
    body: JSON.stringify({idToken:idToken}),
```

```
    headers: new Headers({
       'Content-Type': 'application/json'
    })
  }).then(res => res.json())
  .catch(error => console.error('Error:', error))
  .then(res => {
    console.log(res,"after token valid");
  firebase.auth().signInWithCustomToken(res.customToken).catch(function(error
  ) {
       var errorCode = error.code;
       var errorMessage = error.message;
    });
  })
```

After the successful authentication, the user signed in to our application with account specified by the `uid`, which we included in creating the custom token method.

In the same way, the other Firebase authentication methods works like `signInWithEmailAndPassword()` and `signInWithCredential()`, and the `auth`/`request.auth` object will be available in Firebase Realtime database security rules with the user `uid`. In the preceding example, we specified why to generate the custom token.

```
//Firebase Realtime Database Rules
{
  "rules": {
  "admin": {
  ".read": "auth.uid === 'guest_user'"
  }
  }
}

//Google Cloud Storage Rules
service firebase.storage {
 match /b/<firebase-storage-bucket-name>/o {
 match /admin/{filename} {
 allow read, write: if request.auth.uid == "guest_user";
 }
 }
}
```

In the same way, we can also access the additional passed objects, which are available in `auth.token` and `request.auth.token`:

```
//Firebase Realtime Database Rules
{
 "rules": {
 "subscribeServices": {
 ".read": "auth.token.paid === true"
 }
 }
}

service firebase.storage {
 match /b/<firebase-storage-bucket-name>/o {
 match /subscribeServices/{filename} {
 allow read, write: if request.auth.token.paid === true;
 }
 }
}
```

Firebase can also provide us the way to get the `uid` once the user logged into the app; it creates a corresponding ID token that uniquely identifies them, and we can send this token to the server for verifying and give them access to several resources of the application. For example, when we create a custom backend server to communicate with an app, we might need to identify the currently signed-in user on that server securely using HTTPS.

To retrieve the ID token from Firebase, ensure that the user has signed in to the application, and we can use the following method to retrieve the ID token in your react application:

```
firebase.auth().currentUser.getIdToken(/* forceRefresh */
true).then(function(idToken) {
 // Send this token to custom backend server via HTTPS
}).catch(function(error) {
 // Handle error
});
```

Once we have this ID token, we can send this JWT (JSON Web Token) to backend server Firebase Admin SDK or any third-party library to validate it.

For validating and decoding the ID token, Firebase Admin SDK has a built-in `verifyIdToken(idToken)` method; if the provided token is not expired, valid, and properly signed, this method returns the decoded ID token:

```
function validateToken(req,res){
  const idToken= req.body.idToken;
  admin.auth().verifyIdToken(idToken)
   .then(function(decodedToken) {
   var uid = decodedToken.uid;
  //...
  }).catch(function(error) {
  // Handle error
  });
}
```

Now, let's extend our existing application where the user can see only those tickets that they have submitted, and we'll also give the ability to the user to update the existing profile. We'll also create an admin panel in React and, based on the role, we show the admin UI to the user.

Custom claims for admin access and security rules

As we saw earlier, Firebase Admin SDK supports defining custom attributes with the token. These custom attributes give the ability to define different levels of access, including role-based control to the app, which is enforced in an application's security rules.

We need to define the user roles in the following common cases:

- Giving a user the admin role for accessing the resources
- Assigning different groups to the user
- Giving a user multi-level access such as Paid, Regular user, Managers, Support Team, and such

We can also define the rules based on the database where we need give limited access, such as we have database node `helpdesk/tickets/all`, where all the data tickets' data can be accessed. However, we want only the admin user to be able to see the all the tickets. To achieve this objective more efficiently, verify the email ID and add the custom user claim named admin with the following Realtime Database rule:

```
{
  "rules": {
   "helpdesk":{
    "tickets":{
```

```
    "all": {
      ".read": "auth.token.admin === true",
      ".write": "auth.token.admin === true",
      }
     }
    }
   }
  }
```

 Do not confuse Custom claims with Custom Authentication and Firebase Authentication. It applies to users already signed in with supported providers (Email/Password, Github, Google, Facebook, phone, and such), but custom authentication is used when we use different authentication, which is not supported by Firebase. For example, a user signed in with Firebase Auth's Email/Password provider can have access control defined using custom claims.

Adding custom claim with Admin SDK

In the Firebase Admin SDK, we can apply custom claims using the `setCustomUserClaims()` method, which comes built-in with Firebase:

```
admin.auth().setCustomUserClaims(uid, {admin: true}).then(() => {
});
```

Verifying custom claim with Admin SDK sending the app

Firebase Admin SDK also provides us the method to verify the token using the `verifyIdToken()` method:

```
admin.auth().verifyIdToken(idToken).then((claims) => {
  if (claims.admin === true) {
    // Allow access to admin resource.
  }
});
```

We can also check whether the custom claim is available or not in the user object:

```
admin.auth().getUser(uid).then((userRecord) => {
    console.log(userRecord.customClaims.admin);
});
```

Now, let's see how we can implement this in our existing application.

First, let's create a restful API in the Node Admin SDK backend server:

```
app.post('/setCustomClaims', (req, res) => {
// Get the ID token passed by the client app.
const idToken = req.body.idToken;
console.log("accepted", idToken, req.body);
// Verify the ID token
admin.auth().verifyIdToken(idToken).then((claims) => {
// Verify user is eligible for admin access or not
if (typeof claims.email !== 'undefined' &&
claims.email.indexOf('@adminhelpdesk.com') != -1) {
// Add custom claims for admin access.
admin.auth().setCustomUserClaims(claims.sub, {
admin: true,
}).then(function() {
// send back to the app to refresh token and shows the admin UI.
res.send(JSON.stringify({
status: 'success',
role:'admin'
}));
});
} else if (typeof claims.email !== 'undefined'){
// Add custom claims for admin access.
admin.auth().setCustomUserClaims(claims.sub, {
admin: false,
}).then(function() {
// Tell client to refresh token on user.
res.send(JSON.stringify({
status: 'success',
role:'employee'
}));
});
}
else{
// return nothing
res.send(JSON.stringify({status: 'ineligible'}));
}
})
});
```

I have manually created one admin user with `harmeet@adminhelpdesk.com` in Firebase Console with help of admin SDK; we need to verify and add the custom claims for admin.

Now, open `App.JSX` and add the following code snippet; set the initial state of the application based on the role:

```
constructor() {
super();
this.state = {
  authenticated : false,
  data:'',
  userUid:'',
    role:{
      admin:false,
      type:''
    }
  }
}
```

Now, calling the preceding API in the `componentWillMount()` component lifecycle method we need to get the `idToken` from user object from `firebase.auth().onAuthStateChanged((user))` and send it to the server for verification:

```
this.getIdToken(user).then((idToken)=>{
 console.log(idToken);
 fetch('http://localhost:3000/setCustomClaims', {
   method: 'POST', // or 'PUT'
   body: JSON.stringify({idToken:idToken}),
   headers: new Headers({
     'Content-Type': 'application/json'
   })
}).then(res => res.json())
 .catch(error => console.error('Error:', error))
 .then(res => {
 console.log(res,"after token valid");
 if(res.status === 'success' && res.role === 'admin'){
    firebase.auth().currentUser.getIdToken(true);
     this.setState({
       authenticated:true,
       data:user.providerData,
       userUid:user.uid,
         role:{
           admin:true,
           type:'admin'
         }
     })
 }
 else if (res.status === 'success' && res.role === 'employee'){
 this.setState({
```

```
        authenticated:true,
        data:user.providerData,
        userUid:user.uid,
        role:{
            admin:false,
            type:'employee'
            }
        })
    }
    else{
        ToastDanger('Invalid Token !!')
    }
```

In the preceding code, we are using the `fetch` API to send the HTTP request. It's similar to XMLHttpRequest, but it has the new feature and is more powerful. Based on the response, we are setting the state of the component and registering the component into the router.

This is how our router component looks:

```
{
  this.state.authenticated && !this.state.role.admin
  ?
  (
  <React.Fragment>
  <Route path="/view-ticket" render={() => (
  <ViewTicketTable userId = {this.state.userUid} />
  )}/>
  <Route path="/add-ticket" render={() => (
  <AddTicketForm userId = {this.state.userUid} userInfo = {this.state.data}
  />
  )}/>
  <Route path="/user-profile" render={() => (
  <ProfileUpdateForm userId = {this.state.userUid} userInfo =
  {this.state.data} />
  )}/>
  </React.Fragment>
  )
  :
  (
  <React.Fragment>
    <Route path="/get-alluser" component = { AppUsers }/>
    <Route path="/tickets" component = { GetAllTickets }/>
    <Route path="/add-new-user" component = { NewUserForm }/>
  </React.Fragment>
  )
  }
```

Here's the list of components that we are registering and rendering admin component if the user is an admin:

- `AppUser`: To get the list of user for application, which is also responsible for deleting the user and searching the user by different criteria
- `Tickets`: To see the list of all tickets and change the status of the ticket
- `NewUserForm`: To add the new user to the application

We are performing the preceding operation with Node.js Firebase Admin SDK server.

Create a folder with the name of `admin` and create a file in it, called `getAllUser.jsx`. In that, we will create a React component, which is responsible for fetching and displaying the list of the user into UI; we'll also add the functionality of searching the user by different criteria, such as email ID, phone number, and more.

In the `getAllUser.jsx` file, this is how our render method looks:

```
<form className="form-inline">
//Search Input
    <div className="form-group" style={marginRight}>
        <input type="text" id="search" className="form-control"
        placeholder="Search user" value={this.state.search} required
        />
    </div>
//Search by options
    <select className="form-control" style={marginRight}>
        <option value="email">Search by Email</option>
        <option value="phone">Search by Phone Number</option>
    </select>
    <button className="btn btn-primary btn-sm">Search</button>
</form>
```

We have also added the table in the `render` method to display the list of users:

```
<tbody>
{
this.state.users.length > 0 ?
this.state.users.map((list,index) => {
return (
<tr key={list.uid}>
<td>{list.email}</td>
<td>{list.displayName}</td>
<td>{list.metadata.lastSignInTime}</td>
<td>{list.metadata.creationTime}</td>
<td>
    <button className="btn btn-sm btn-primary" type="button"
```

```
style={marginRight} onClick={()=>
{this.deleteUser(list.uid)}}>Delete User</button>
        <button className="btn btn-sm btn-primary" type="button"
onClick={()=>                            {this.viewProfile(list.uid)}}>View
Profile</button>
 </td>
 </tr>
 )
 }) :
 <tr>
    <td colSpan="5" className="text-center">No users found.</td>
 </tr>
 }
 </tbody>
```

This is the table body, which is displaying the list of users with action buttons, and now we need to call the users API in the `componentDidMount()` method:

```
fetch('http://localhost:3000/users', {
 method: 'GET', // or 'PUT'
 headers: new Headers({
 'Content-Type': 'application/json'
 })
 }).then(res => res.json())
 .catch(error => console.error('Error:', error))
 .then(response => {
 console.log(response,"after token valid");
 this.setState({
   users:response
 })
 console.log(this.state.users,'All Users');
 })
```

Similarly, we need to call other APIs to delete, View User Profile, and search:

```
deleteUser(uid){
 fetch('http://localhost:3000/deleteUser', {
    method: 'POST', // or 'PUT'
    body:JSON.stringify({uid:uid}),
    headers: new Headers({
        'Content-Type': 'application/json'
    })
 }).then(res => res.json())
    .catch(error => console.error('Error:', error))
 }
//Fetch User Profile
 viewProfile(uid){
 fetch('http://localhost:3000/getUserProfile', {
```

```
    method: 'POST', // or 'PUT'
    body:JSON.stringify({uid:uid}),
    headers: new Headers({
        'Content-Type': 'application/json'
    })
}).then(res => res.json())
    .catch(error => console.error('Error:', error))
    .then(response => {
        console.log(response.data,"User Profile");
    })
}
```

For searching, Firebase Admin SDK has built-in methods: `getUserByEmail()` and `getUserByPhoneNumber()`. We can implement these in the same way as `delete()` and `fetch()`, which we created in the Firebase Admin API:

```
//Search User by Email
searchByEmail(emailId){
 fetch('http://localhost:3000/searchByEmail', {
 method: 'POST', // or 'PUT'
 body:JSON.stringify({email:emailId}),
 headers: new Headers({
 'Content-Type': 'application/json'
 })
}).then(res => res.json())
.catch(error => console.error('Error:', error))
.then(response => {
console.log(response.data,"User Profile");
this.setState({
    users:response
})
})
}
```

Look at the following `node.js` API Code Snippet:

```
function listAllUsers(req,res) {
 var nextPageToken;
 // List batch of users, 1000 at a time.
 admin.auth().listUsers(1000,nextPageToken)
 .then(function(data) {
 data = data.users.map((el) => {
 return el.toJSON();
 })
 res.send(data);
 })
 .catch(function(error) {
```

```
  console.log("Error fetching the users from firebase:", error);
  });
}
function deleteUser(req, res){
  const userId = req.body.uid;
  admin.auth().deleteUser(userId)
  .then(function() {
    console.log("Successfully deleted user"+userId);
    res.send({status:"success", msg:"Successfully deleted user"})
  })
  .catch(function(error) {
    console.log("Error deleting user:", error);
  res.send({status:"error", msg:"Error deleting user:"})
  });
}
function searchByEmail(req, res){
  const searchType = req.body.email;
  admin.auth().getUserByEmail(userId)
  .then(function(userInfo) {
    console.log("Successfully fetched user information associated with this
email"+userId);
    res.send({status:"success", data:userInfo})
  })
  .catch(function(error) {
    console.log("Error fetching user info:", error);
  res.send({status:"error", msg:"Error fetching user informaition"})
  });
}
```

Now, we'll create an API to call the preceding functions based on the user's request:

```
app.get('/users', function (req, res) {
 listAllUsers(req,res);
})
app.get('/deleteUser', function (req, res) {
 deleteUser(req,res);
})
app.post('/searchByEmail', function (req, res){
 searchByEmail(req, res)
})
```

Now, let's take a quick look at our application in browser, see how it looks, and try to log in with admin user:

A screenshot of our application when logged in with admin credentials; the purpose is to show the UI and console when we log in as admin

That looks amazing! Just take a look at the preceding screenshot; it's showing different navigation for admin, and if you can see in the console, it's showing the token with custom claim object, which we added to this user to admin access:

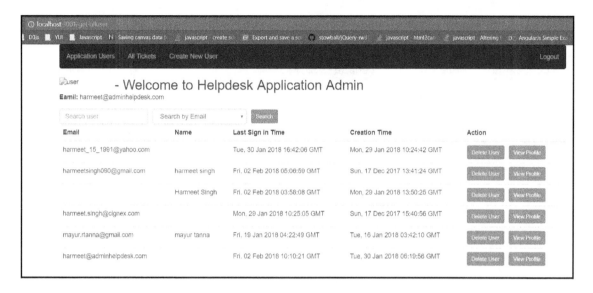

It looks great! We can see the users of the application with action button and search UI.

Now, consider that we delete the user from the listing and, at the same time that user session is active and using the application. In this scenario, we need to manage the session for the user and give the prompt to reauthenticate, because every time the user logs in, the user credentials are sent to the Firebase Authentication backend and exchanged for a Firebase ID token (a JWT) and refresh token.

These are the common scenarios where we need to manage the session of the user:

- User is deleted
- User is disabled
- Email address and password changed

The Firebase Admin SDK also gives the ability to revoke the specific user session using the `revokeRefreshToken()` method. It revokes active refresh tokens of a given user. If we reset the password, Firebase Authentication backend automatically revokes the user token.

Refer to the following code snippet of Firebase Cloud Function to revoke the user based on a specific `uid`:

```
const admin = require('firebase-admin');
admin.initializeApp(functions.config().firebase);
// Revoke all refresh tokens for a specified user for whatever reason.
function revokeUserTokens(uid){
return admin.auth().revokeRefreshTokens(uid)
.then(() => {
    // Get user's tokensValidAfterTime.
    return admin.auth().getUser(uid);
})
.then((userRecord) => {
    // Convert to seconds as the auth_time in the token claims is in
seconds too.
    const utcRevocationTimeSecs = new
Date(userRecord.tokensValidAfterTime).getTime() / 1000;
    // Save the refresh token revocation timestamp. This is needed to track
ID token
    // revocation via Firebase rules.
    const metadataRef = admin.database().ref("metadata/" + userRecord.uid);
    return metadataRef.set({revokeTime: utcRevocationTimeSecs});
 });
}
```

As we know, Firebase ID tokens are stateless JWT, which can only be verified by sending the request to Firebase Authentication backend server to check whether the token's status is revoked or not. For this reason, performing this check on your server is very costly and adds the extra effort, requiring an extra network request load. We can avoid this network request by setting up Firebase Rules that check for revocation, rather than sending the request to the Firebase Admin SDK.

This is the normal way to declare the rules with no client access to write to store revocation time per user:

```
{
"rules": {
    "metadata": {
        "$user_id": {
            ".read": "$user_id === auth.uid",
            ".write": "false",
            }
        }
    }
}
```

However, if we want to allow only unrevoked and authenticated users to access the protected data, we must have the following rule configured:

```
{
  "rules": {
      "users": {
          "$user_id": {
              ".read": "$user_id === auth.uid && auth.token.auth_time >
(root.child('metadata').child(auth.uid).child('revokeTime').val() || 0)",
              ".write": "$user_id === auth.uid && auth.token.auth_time >
(root.child('metadata').child(auth.uid).child('revokeTime').val() || 0)"
          }
      }
  }
}
```

Any time a user's refresh on browser tokens are revoked, the `tokensValidAfterTime` UTC timestamp is saved in the database node.

When a user's ID token is to be verified, the additional check boolean flag has to be passed to the `verifyIdToken()` method. If the user's token is revoked, the user should be signed out from the app or asked to reauthenticate using reauthentication APIs provided by the Firebase Authentication client SDKs.

For example, we created one method above `setCustomClaims` in that method; just add the following code inside the `catch` method:

```
.catch(error => {
    // Invalid token or token was revoked:
    if (error.code == 'auth/id-token-revoked') {
    //Shows the alert to user to reauthenticate
    // Firebase Authentication API gives the API to
reauthenticateWithCredential /reauthenticateWithPopup
/reauthenticateWithRedirect
    }
});
```

Also, if the token is revoked, send the notification to the client app to reauthenticate.

Consider this example for email/password Firebase authentication providers:

```
let password = prompt('Please provide your password for reauthentication');
let credential = firebase.auth.EmailAuthProvider.credential(
firebase.auth().currentUser.email, password);
firebase.auth().currentUser.reauthenticateWithCredential(credential)
.then(result => {
// User successfully reauthenticated.
})
.catch(error => {
// An error occurred.
});
```

Now, let's click on the **All Tickets** link to see the list of tickets submitted by all the users:

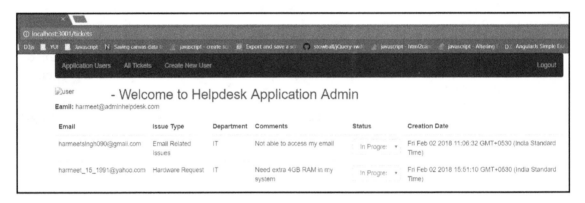

As an admin user, we can change the status of the ticket that will get updated in Firebase Realtime Database. Now if you click on **Create New User**, it will display the form to add user information.

Let's create one new component and add the following code to the render method:

```
<form className="form" onSubmit={this.handleSubmitEvent}>
 <div className="form-group">
 <input type="text" id="name" className="form-control"
 placeholder="Enter Employee Name" value={this.state.name} required
onChange={this.handleChange} />
 </div>
 <div className="form-group">
 <input type="text" id="email" className="form-control"
 placeholder="Employee Email ID" value={this.state.email} required
onChange={this.handleChange} />
 </div>
 <div className="form-group">
 <input type="password" id="password" className="form-control"
 placeholder="Application Password" value={this.state.password} required
onChange={this.handleChange} />
 </div>
 <div className="form-group">
 <input type="text" id="phoneNumber" className="form-control"
 placeholder="Employee Phone Number" value={this.state.phoneNumber}
 required onChange={this.handleChange} />
 </div>
 <div className="form-group">
 <input
 type="file"
 ref={input => {
 this.fileInput = input;
 }}
 />
 </div>
 <button className="btn btn-primary btn-sm">Submit</button>
 </form>
```

On `handleSubmitEvent(e)`, we need to call the `createNewUser()` Firebase admin SDK method, passing the form data into it:

```
e.preventDefault();
 //React form data object
 var data = {
 email:this.state.email,
 emailVerified: false,
 password:this.state.password,
 displayName:this.state.name,
 phoneNumber:this.state.phoneNumber,
 profilePhoto:this.fileInput.files[0],
 disabled: false
```

```
}
fetch('http://localhost:3000/createNewUser', {
  method: 'POST', // or 'PUT'
  body:JSON.stringify({data:data}),
  headers: new Headers({
  'Content-Type': 'application/json'
})
}).then(res => res.json())
.catch(error => {
ToastDanger(error)
})
.then(response => {
ToastSuccess(response.msg)
});
```

Start the server again and open the application in your browser. Let's try to create the new user in our application with admin credentials:

Create New User component; the purpose of the image is to show the alert message when we fill the form and submit to the Firebase to create a new user

That looks awesome; we have successfully created the new user in our application and returned the automatic generated `uid` by Firebase for a new user.

Now, let's move on further and log in with a normal user:

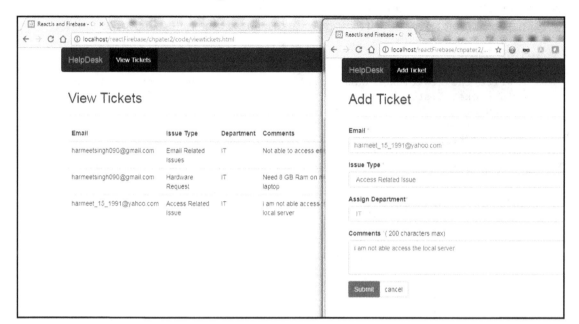

If you take a look at the preceding screenshot, once we logged into the app using any Firebase Auth provider, on the dashboard, it shows all the tickets of the users, but it should only display the ones associated with this email ID. For this, we need to change the data structure and Firebase node ref.

This is the most important part of the application where we need to plan how data will be saved and retrieved to make the process as easy as possible.

How data is structured in a JSON tree

In Firebase Realtime Database, all data is stored as JSON objects, which is a cloud-hosted JSON tree. When we add data to the database, it becomes a node in the existing JSON structure with an associated key, which is autogenerated by Firebase. We can also provide our own custom keys, such as user IDs or any semantic names, or they can be provided using the `push()` method.

For example, in our Helpdesk Application, we are storing the tickets at a path, such as /helpdesk/tickets; now we'll replace this with /helpdesk/tickets/$uid/$ticketKey. Take a look at the following code:

```
var newTicketKey =
firebase.database().ref('/helpdesk').child('tickets').push().key;
  // Write the new ticket data simultaneously in the tickets list and the
user's ticket list.
  var updates = {};
  updates['/helpdesk/tickets/' + userId + '/' + newTicketKey] = data;
  updates['/helpdesk/tickets/all/'+ newTicketKey] = data;
```

This is how data structure looks for creating and retrieving the tickets from the database:

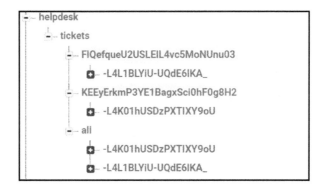

In the preceding image, the highlighted node is $uid, which belongs to the user who has submitted the ticket.

This is how our full code looks:

```
var newTicketKey =
firebase.database().ref('/helpdesk').child('tickets').push().key;
  // Write the new ticket data simultaneously in the tickets list and the
user's ticket list.
  var updates = {};
  updates['/helpdesk/tickets/' + userId + '/' + newTicketKey] = data;
  updates['/helpdesk/tickets/all/'+ newTicketKey] = data;

  return firebase.database().ref().update(updates).then(()=>{
  ToastSuccess("Saved Successfully!!");
  this.setState({
      issueType:"",
      department:"",
      comment:""
  });
```

```
}).catch((error)=>{
    ToastDanger(error.message);
});
```

Open the browser and submit the ticket again; now look at the ticket dashboard:

It looks great! Now the user can only see the tickets they have submitted. In the next chapter, we'll see how we can apply security rules and common security threats in our data in the database.

Summary

This chapter explained how we can configure and initialize the Firebase Admin SDK to create our app backend in NodeJS. It also explained how we can manage our app users using User Management API of Firebase Admin without going to Firebase Console, such as the following:

- Create
- Delete
- Update
- Remove

Firebase Admin SDK gives us the power to create and verify the Custom JWT tokens, which allow the user to authenticate with any provider, even if it's not available in the Firebase Auth Providers list. It also gives you the power to manage the user's session in case of any change in user information, such as the user is deleted, disabled, the email address or password is changed, and more.

We also learned how we can control the access to custom claims. This helps us provide the ability to implement role-based access control to give users different levels of access (roles), in Firebase apps.

In the next chapter, we will learn the database security risks and the checklist to prevent such threats. We will also see the security part of Firebase Realtime Database and the Firebase Realtime Database Rules language.

Firebase Security and Rules

6

In the previous chapter, we saw how we can incorporate access management in an application to secure it from unauthorized access, which is essentially the application level security. However, what if we don't have our database secured? Well, in that case, data can be misused by unauthorized users or even authorized users, such as database administrators, which leads to business loss or sometimes legal actions.

Data security is always a major concern, especially when it is hosted on Cloud Server. We have to protect our data against the compromises of integrity, availability, and confidentiality. It doesn't matter whether you are using RDBMS, such as MySQL or MSSQL, or NoSQL, such as MongoDB or Firebase Realtime Database; all these databases have to be secured by restricting access to the data. In this chapter, we will briefly look at the common database security risks and the checklist to prevent such threats. We will also see the security part of Firebase Realtime Database and the Firebase Realtime Database Rules language.

Here's a list of the topics we will discuss in this chapter:

- Overview of common Database Security Risks and Preventive measures
- Overview of Firebase Security
- Overview of Firebase Realtime Database Rules
- Structure and Definition of Firebase Realtime Database Rules
- Introduction to Data Indexing
- Database Backups and Restore

Let's start with Security Risks and Prevention of the threats.

Security risks and prevention

The databases are at the heart of any organization since they contain customers' data and confidential business data and hence they are targeted by hackers very often. There are some common threats identified over the last few years and they include these:

- Unauthorized or unintended activity
- Malware Infections
- Physical damage to database servers
- Data corruption due to invalid data
- Performance Degradation

To prevent such risks, there are many protocols or security standards that need to be followed:

1. **Access Control**: It includes Authentication and Authorization. All the database systems provide access control mechanisms such as authentication with username and password for authentication. At the same time, in some of the databases, it is not mandatory to set it and hence sometimes people don't enable it, leaving the database insecure. Similarly, in all databases, authorization mechanisms such as role-based security is provided to restrict the users to certain data or database. However, people sometimes give root or admin access to all the users, leaving the data open to all the users.

2. **Auditing**: Auditing involves monitoring of database activities performed by all users for enhanced security and protection of data. Many of the database platforms include inbuilt auditing capabilities, which allow you to trace the data creation, deletion, or modification activities and database usage to detect any suspicious activities at an early stage.

3. **Backups**: Backups are meant to recover data from an earlier time and to recover data in case of data deletion or data corruption. Depending on the requirement, the backup process can be automated or manual. Ideally, it should be automated so that regular backups can be taken. While it is worth to have at least a few backups, the data storage space can be significant, depending on the size of your data/backup. To reduce the size of backups, backup files should be compressed before persisting them.

4. **Data Integrity Controls**: Data Integrity refers to the consistency and accuracy of the data stored in the database. Data validation is prerequisite for data integrity. Many Relational Databases (RDBMS) enforce data integrity through constraints like a Primary key and Foreign Key constraints. In case of NoSQL, data validation at the database level, and also at the application level, is required for data integrity.

5. **Application level security**: Application level security is also required to prevent any inappropriate data from being saved on the database. Generally, developers have validations at form level and also at the business, to ensure that they save valid data in the database.

6. **Encryption**: It is very important to encrypt personal data such as SSN or financial data such as Credit card information to prevent its misuse. Usually, SSL encryption is used to encrypt the connection between client and server, which is essentially network level security, to prevent any malicious attacker from reading this information.

Now, let's check how secure our data is in Firebase.

How secure is your Firebase?

Firebase is on cloud storage, so obviously, people think whether it is secure enough. However, there's nothing to worry, as Firebase provides a secured architecture and a set of tools to manage the security of your app. Firebase is hosted on SSL (Secure Sockets Layer), which typically encrypts the connection between client and server and hence prevents any data theft or manipulation at the network layer. Firebase comes with an expression-based rule language that allows you to manage data security by just doing configuration.

Firebase security is all about the configuration over convention so that your application's security-related logic is separate from your business logic. In this way, it makes your application loosely coupled.

In this chapter, we will learn about Firebase Realtime Database security and rules.

Realtime Database Rules Overview

Firebase Database Rules allow you to manage the read and write access permissions to your database. They also help you define how your data will be validated, such as whether it has valid datatype and format. If your rules allow, only then will read and write requests be completed. By default, your rules are set to allow only authenticated users with full read and write access to your database.

Firebase Database Rules have a JavaScript-like syntax and come in four types:

`.read`	It determines whether data is allowed to be read by users and when.
`.write`	It determines whether data is allowed to be written by users and when.
`.validate`	It validates whether a value is correctly formatted, has child attributes, and its data type.
`.indexOn`	It determines whether an index exists on a child to support faster querying and ordering.

You can access and set your rules from the **Database** || **Rules** tab in your Firebase Console:

There are three steps to Firebase Realtime Database security:

1. Authentication of users
2. Authorization of users - control access to data
3. Validation of user inputs

Authentication

User authentication is the first step to secure your application from unauthenticated access. Identifying the user in the first step automatically implies the restriction on data they can access and manipulate. In the applications where we use backend technologies such as Java, Microsoft.Net, or any other platform, we write authentication logic to restrict the access to our application. However, since Firebase is widely used with client-side only applications, we will not have the luxury of backend tools. Luckily, Firebase platform provides an Authentication mechanism—Firebase Authentication—which has built-in support for common authentication mechanisms such as form-based authentication with username and password, Google and Facebook login, and many more. In Chapter 3, *Authentication with Firebase*, and Chapter 5, *User Profile and Access Management*, we have already seen how we can implement the Firebase Authentication. The following rule specifies that to access the database, a user must be authenticated. It also specifies that once a user is authenticated, it can access all the data available in the database:

```
{
  "rules": {
    ".read": "auth != null",
    ".write": "auth != null"
  }
}
```

Authorization

Once the user is authenticated, they can access the database. However, you need some control over who can access what. Everybody should not be allowed to read/write all the data present in your database. This is where Authorization comes into the picture. Firebase Database Rules allow you to control access for each user. Firebase security rules are node based and are managed by a single JSON object that you can edit on your Realtime Database console or using the Firebase CLI:

```
{
  "rules": {
      "users": {
```

```
                   ".read": "true",
                   ".write": "false"
              }
          }
      }
```

The preceding rules determine that all the users will be able to read the users' data but nobody will be able to write to it. Also, note that it is mandatory to have `rules` as the first node in your security JSON object.

Here's an example of a rule that specifies data private to a user:

```
{
   "rules": {
      "users": {
         "$uid": {
            ".read": "$uid === auth.uid",
            ".write": "$uid === auth.uid"
         }
      }
   }
}
```

Now, you might have a question like we have nested data structure, how will the rules apply to that data. To answer that question, one of the points to remember here is that the `.read` and `.write` rules **cascade** meaning; granting a read or write access to a *parent node* always grants that read/write access to *all child nodes*.

 The rules at parent node have higher priority and hence they will override the rules defined at its child level.

Firebase rules also provide some built-in variables and functions that allow you to access Firebase authentication information, refer to other paths, and more. We will check this in detail in the coming sections of this chapter.

Data validation

As seen in the introduction section, we need to validate our data before saving it in the database to maintain data integrity and correctness. Firebase rules provide `.validate` expressions such as `.read` and `.write` to implement validation logic such as length of the field should be only this many characters or it must be of string data type.

Consider this example:

```
{
  "rules": {
      "users": {
          "email": {
              ".validate": "newData.isString() &&
newData.val().length < 50"
          }
      }
  }
}
```

The preceding validation rule for email field determines that the value of email field must be String and its length should be less than 30 characters.

It is important to note that **validation rules do not cascade**, so in order for the write to be allowed, all relevant validation rules must evaluate to true.

Now since we have a basic understanding of Firebase rules, let's deep dive into rules configuration.

Rule definition and structure

Firebase rules provide predefined variables that can be used inside a rule definition:

Name	Definition / Usage
auth	It represents information of the authenticated user. It will be null for an unauthenticated user. It is an object that contains uid, token, and provider fields and corresponding values.
$ variables	It represents wildcard path to refer to the dynamically generated keys and represent IDs.
root	It represents data snapshot at the root path in the Firebase database before applying the given database operation.
data	It represents the Data Snapshot before applying the given database operation. For example, in case of the update or write, the root represents the original data snapshot without the changes in the update or write.
newData	It represents the Data Snapshot before applying the given database operation. However, it includes both the existing data as well as the new data, which includes data manipulated by the given data operation.

now	It represents current time in milliseconds—the number of *seconds* that have elapsed *since* January 1, *1970* (midnight UTC).

In the following section, we'll look at how we can use these predefined variables in our rules.

As we saw in the Authorization section, we need to see how rules will apply to the nested data. A rule of thumb is that we need to structure rules based on the structure of the data in the database.

We will extend our HelpDesk application developed in `chapter 5`, *User Profile and Access Management,* of this book.

We have a data structure as follows:

```
"helpdesk" : {
    "tickets" : {
        "FlQefqueU2USLElL4vc5MoNUnu03" : {
            "-L4L1BLYiU-UQdE6lKA_" : {
                "comments" : "Need extra 4GB RAM in my system",
                "date" : "Fri Feb 02 2018 15:51:10 GMT+0530 (India Standard
                    Time)",
                "department" : "IT",
                "email" : "harmeet_15_1991@yahoo.com",
                "issueType" : "Hardware Request",
                "status" : "progress"
            }
        },
        "KEEyErkmP3YE1BagxSci0hF0g8H2" : {
            "-L4K01hUSDzPXTIXY9oU" : {
                "comments" : "Not able to access my email",
                "date" : "Fri Feb 02 2018 11:06:32 GMT+0530 (India Standard
                    Time)",
                "department" : "IT",
                "email" : "harmeetsingh090@gmail.com",
                "issueType" : "Email Related Issues",
                "status" : "progress"
            }
        },
        "all" : {
            "-L4K01hUSDzPXTIXY9oU" : {
                "comments" : "Not able to access my email",
                "date" : "Fri Feb 02 2018 11:06:32 GMT+0530 (India Standard
                    Time)",
                "department" : "IT",
                "email" : "harmeetsingh090@gmail.com",
```

```
      "issueType" : "Email Related Issues",
      "status" : "progress"
    },
    "-L4L1BLYiU-UQdE6lKA_" : {
      "comments" : "Need extra 4GB RAM in my system",
      "date" : "Fri Feb 02 2018 15:51:10 GMT+0530 (India Standard
        Time)",
      "department" : "IT",
      "email" : "harmeet_15_1991@yahoo.com",
      "issueType" : "Hardware Request",
      "status" : "progress"
    }
  }
 }
}
```

Here, we can see that to have data to be secured at the user level, to show only the tickets relevant to the logged in user, we are storing them under **userId**, such as FlQefqueU2USLElL4vc5MoNUnu03 and KEEyErkmP3YE1BagxSci0hF0g8H2, and to show all the tickets to admin, we are storing them under all. However, this is not the ideal solution, since it has two issues: data is redundant, and to update any data, we will have to update it at two places. Luckily, we can handle this kind of security directly in the database with Rules.

We will change our data, and we will remove the all node from data. We will also add one variable under $userId to identify whether a user is an admin or not. So it will look like this:

```
"helpdesk" : {
    "tickets" : {
        "FlQefqueU2USLElL4vc5MoNUnu03" : {
            "-L4L1BLYiU-UQdE6lKA_" : {
                "comments" : "Need extra 4GB RAM in my system",
                "date" : "Fri Feb 02 2018 15:51:10 GMT+0530 (India Standard
                  Time)",
                "department" : "IT",
                "email" : "harmeet_15_1991@yahoo.com",
                "issueType" : "Hardware Request",
                "status" : "progress"
            },
            "isAdmin": true
        },
        "KEEyErkmP3YE1BagxSci0hF0g8H2" : {
            "-L4K01hUSDzPXTIXY9oU" : {
                "comments" : "Not able to access my email",
                "date" : "Fri Feb 02 2018 11:06:32 GMT+0530 (India Standard
```

```
          Time)",
          "department" : "IT",
          "email" : "harmeetsingh090@gmail.com",
          "issueType" : "Email Related Issues",
          "status" : "progress"
        },
        "isAdmin": false
      }
    }
  }
}
```

Our rules will look as follows:

```
{
  "rules": {
    "helpdesk": {
      "tickets": {
        ".read": "data.child(auth.uid).child('isAdmin').val()==true",
        ".write": "data.child(auth.uid).child('isAdmin').val()==true",
        "$uid": {
          ".read": "auth.uid == $uid",
          ".write": "auth.uid == $uid"
        }
      }
    }
  }
}
```

These rules essentially impose restrictions that if the user is Admin, that is, `isAdmin` is true, then they can read and write all the data. However, other users will only be able to read/write their own data.

Here, we have also used predefined variable data, which represents the `DataSnapshot` before applying a `write` operation. Similarly, we can use the `root` variable to refer to the root path and `newData` to refer to the data snapshot that will exist after a write operation.

Now, if you have observed, we have used `.child`, which is essentially used to refer to any child path/attribute. In our rule, we are checking that under `$uid`, the value of `isAdmin` is true, since we want to give access to all data to an admin. Similarly, we can use any data as a condition in our rules.

Also, an important thing to note here is that once we have defined `.read` and `.write` rules at parent level `tickets`, we are not checking the `isAdmin` condition under `$uid`, because **rules do cascade**, so once you have granted read/write permissions to admins, you don't need to repeat those conditions at the `$uid` level. At the same time, it is important to note that it is mandatory to have a rule defined at a parent location. If we don't define them at the parent location, your data operation will fail completely even though the child path is accessible.

For example, in the following rule, we can see that though we have access permissions at ticket level, we won't be able to access data since we haven't defined rules at `$uid` level:

```
{
  "rules": {
    "helpdesk": {
      "tickets": {
        "$ticketId": {
          ".read": true,
          ".write": true
        }
      }
    }
  }
}
```

Query-based rules

As seen in the preceding example, rules can't be used as filters. However, at times, we need to give access to only subsets of data based on some conditions or query parameters. For example, let's say that we need to return only the first 100 records out of 1000 records from the query result set. We can achieve this through the use of the **query.** expressions to give read and write access to your result set based on the query parameters:

```
tickets: {
  ".read": "query.limitToFirst <= 100"
}
```

The preceding will give access to the first 100 records that are ordered by key by default. If you want to specify `orderByChild`, you can also do that, as follows:

```
tickets: {
  ".read": "query.orderByChild == 'department' && query.limitToFirst <=
100"
}
```

Ensure that when you read the data, you specify `orderByChild`, otherwise your read will fail.

Data indexing

Firebase allows you to write queries using child keys. To improve your query performance, you can define an index on those keys using the `.indexOn` rule. We assume that you already knew how the index works as almost all database systems support index.

Let's take an example to understand this better. Let's say that in our **HelpDesk** system, we often order tickets by department key, and we are using `orderbyChild()`:

```
{
  "rules": {
    "helpdesk": {
        "tickets": {
            ".indexOn": ["department"]
          }
        }
      }
    }
```

Similarly, if we are using `orderByValue()`, we can have the following rule:

```
".indexOn": ".value"
```

Backups

In the first section of this chapter, we saw how important it is to manage the backups of the data. Though you can take and maintain your data backups manually, there are chances that you miss out something and lose the backups. Fortunately, Firebase provides an automatic backup service that can be set up to take automatic backups of your data and rules daily. Note that this service is only available to Blaze plan users and will be chargeable as per Standard rates. You can check various subscription plans available at `https://firebase.google.com/pricing/`.

Setup

You can set up database backups from the **Backups** tab of the Realtime Database of Firebase section. The setup wizard will guide you through the steps to configure automatic backups. Your Database backup activity will happen at a specific hour each day without affecting the load and ensures the highest availability for all backup customers.

Additionally, you can also take a manual backup whenever you want to get a point in time snapshot of your data and rules.

Your backups will be stored in Google Cloud Storage, which is an object storage service provided by Google Cloud Platform. Essentially, Google Cloud Storage provides buckets that are like directories on computer filesystem, in which your backups will be stored. So, once the setup is done, a bucket will be created with permissions where your Firebase can write the data. We will see Google Cloud Storage and Firebase Cloud Storage in detail in Chapter 8, *Firebase Cloud Storage*.

The backup service automatically compresses the backup files using **Gzip** compression that reduces the overall backup size and ultimately reduces cost and also minimizes data transfer time. The compressed file size varies based on the data in your database, but in general, it reduces the overall file size to 1/3 of the original decompressed file size. You can enable and disable Gzip compression based on your requirements.

To save further cost, you can also you can enable a 30-day lifecycle policy on your bucket to delete older backups; for example, backups older than 30 days automatically get deleted.

Your Gzipped JSON files can be decompressed by executing the following command-line command using the `gunzip` binary, which is available by default on OS-X and most Linux distributions:

```
gunzip <DATABASE_NAME>.json.gz
```

The filenames will be generated based on the following naming conventions. It will have a timestamp (ISO 8601 Standard):

```
Database data: YYYY-MM-DDTHH:MM:SSZ_<DATABASE_NAME>_data.json
Database rules: YYYY-MM-DDTHH:MM:SSZ_<DATABASE_NAME>_rules.json
```

If you have Gzip compression enabled, the name will be appended by a `.gz` suffix.

Consider this example:

```
Database data: YYYY-MM-DDTHH:MM:SSZ_<DATABASE_NAME>_data.json.gz
Database rules: YYYY-MM-DDTHH:MM:SSZ_<DATABASE_NAME>_rules.json.gz
```

Once you have taken a backup, you would want to restore it at some point in time. Let's check how we can restore the data from a backup.

Restoring from backups

To restore the data from backup, first download the backup file from Google Cloud Storage and decompress it as per the preceding command. Once you have the JSON file, you can import data in either of the two ways:

- Under the database section of Firebase console, you will find an **Import JSON** button that will allow you to upload the file.
- You can use a CURL command: `curl 'https://<DATABASE_NAME>.firebaseio.com/.json?auth=<SECRET>&print=silent' -x PUT -d @<DATABASE_NAME>.json`. Note that you need to replace `DATABASE_NAME` and `SECRET`, respectively, with your own values. You can get the secret from the database settings page.

Summary

This chapter explains the common security threats to data, especially when it resides on cloud, and how we can secure our data. It also explains that Firebase is secure and we shouldn't worry much about the security of data as far as we manage the security properly at our end by defining proper rules in database and control access to the data to the authorized users.

Firebase is hosted on Secure Server Layer, which manages the security at the transport layer. It also gives you a powerful yet simple Rule engine that can be configured to secure your data and, at the same time, give the benefit of separation of concern—separates security logic from application logic.

We also learned in detail about security rules and how we can define them using simple JavaScript-like syntax.

In the next chapter, we will explore Firebase Cloud Messaging and Cloud Functions.

7
Using Firebase Cloud Messaging and Cloud Functions with React

In the previous chapters, we explored some of the Firebase products, such as Realtime Database, Authentication, Cloud Firestore, and Cloud Storage. However, we haven't seen some of the advanced features yet, such as Realtime messaging and serverless app development. Now we are ready to explore them, so let's discuss two more products from Firebase platform: Firebase Cloud Messaging and Cloud Functions. Firebase Cloud Messaging is a messaging platform to send free messages across different platforms: Android, iOS, and web. Cloud Functions allow you to have serverless apps, meaning that you can run your custom application logic without a server.

Here's a list of topics that we'll focus on in this chapter:

- Key features of **Firebase Cloud Messaging (FCM)**
- Setup of Firebase for Javascript Web App
- Client app setup to receive notifications
- Server setup to send the notifications
- Key features of Cloud Functions
- Setup of Firebase SDK for Cloud Functions
- Life cycle of a Cloud Function
- Triggering functions
- Deployment and execution of a function
- Termination of a function

Let's first start with FCM, and then we will go through the Cloud Functions.

Firebase Cloud Messaging (FCM)

FCM provides a platform that helps you send the messages and notifications to the app user in real-time using service workers. You can send hundreds of billions of messages per day for free across different platforms: Android, iOS, and web (Javascript). You can also schedule the message delivery, immediately or in future.

There are two main components in FCM implementation: a trusted environment that includes an app server or a Cloud function to send the messages, and an iOS, Android, or web (JavaScript) client app that receives the messages.

If you know about the **Google Cloud Messaging** (**GCM**), you might have a question of how FCM is different from GCM. The answer to this question is that FCM is the latest and improved version of GCM. It inherits all the infrastructure of GCM and carries improvements for the simplified client development. Just note that GCM is not deprecated and Google is still supporting it. However, the new client-side features will only come to FCM and hence as per Google recommendation, you should upgrade from GCM to FCM.

Though it supports different platforms, Android, iOS, and Web, we will mainly talk about web (Javascript) in this chapter. Let's now look at the key features of FCM.

Key features of FCM

The key features of GCM include Downstream messages, Upstream Messages, and Versatile messaging. Let's see what these feature are in brief in the next section.

Sending downstream messages

The downstream messages are sent to users from the server on behalf of a client app. FCM messages can be divided into two categories: Notification Messages and Data Messages. The notification messages are directly displayed to user. Some examples of the notification messages are alert messages, chat messages, or messages to notify client app to start some processing; let's message backups. The data messages need to be handled in your client app code. Some examples are chat messages or any messages specific to your app. We will talk more about these message types in the next section of FCM Messages.

Sending upstream messages

The upstream messages are sent back from devices to the server via an FCM channel. You can send acknowledgments, chat messages, and other messages from devices back to your server over a reliable FCM channel.

Versatile message targeting

FCM is quite flexible and allows you to send the messages to the target audience on a single device, a group of devices, or to all the subscribers who listen to a topic.

FCM messages

Using FCM, you can send two types of messages to the clients: Notification Messages and Data Messages. The maximum payload size for both kinds of messages is 4 KB when using Firebase SDK. However, when you send messages from the Firebase console, it enforces a 1024 character limit.

The notification messages are handled by FCM SDK automatically, since they are just display messages. You can use notification messages when you want FCM to display a notification on your client app's behalf. Notification messages contain a predefined set of keys and can also contain an optional data payload.

The notification message object looks like this:

```
{
  "message":{
    "token":"bk3RNwTe3H0:CI2k_HHwgIpoDKCIZvvDMExUdFQ3P1...",
    "notification":{
      "title":"This is an FCM notification message!",
      "body":"FCM message"
    }
  }
}
```

The data messages are handled by a client app and contain the user-defined keys. They look as follows:

```
{
  "message":{
    "token":"bk3RNwTe3H0:CI2k_HHwgIpoDKCIZvvDMExUdFQ3P1...",
    "data":{
      "Name" : "MT",
      "Education" : "Ph.D."
    }
  }
}
```

We will see what a token is in the upcoming sections.

Setup of Firebase for Javascript web app

FCM allows you to receive notification messages in your web application running in different browsers with the support of service worker. The service worker is a browser script that runs in the background and provides features such as offline data capability, background data syncing, push notifications, and more. The service worker support is available in the following browsers:

- Chrome: 50+
- Firefox: 44+
- Opera Mobile: 37+

Using service workers, people can carry out some malicious activities, such as filtering the responses or hijacking connections. To avoid that, service workers can only be used on pages served over HTTPS. Hence, you will need a valid SSL certificate on your server if you want to use FCM. Note that in the local environment, you don't need SSL; it works at localhost without any issues.

Installing Firebase and Firebase CLI

If you are starting with a new React project, the easiest way to get started is with the React Starter Kit. You can create a React project using the following command and then install **firebase** and **firebase-tools**. If it is an existing React and Firebase project, you can skip the installation steps:

```
npm install -g create-react-app
```

You can install Firebase using the following command:

```
npm install firebase --save
```

You will also need to install the Firebase CLI to run your project on a server. It can be installed using the following command:

```
npm install -g firebase-tools
```

Now, we will extend the Helpdesk application with FCM implementation.

Configuring the browser to receive messages

First of all, you will need to add a web app manifest from `https://developers.google.com/web/fundamentals/web-app-manifest/file` in our project and add the following to it:

```
{
  "gcm_sender_id": "103953800507"
}
```

It tells the browser that FCM is allowed to send the messages to this App. The `103953800507` value is hard-coded and must be the same in any of your App. The web app manifest is a simple JSON file and will contain the configuration metadata related to your project, such as the start URL of your App and App icon details.

We have created a `manifest.json` file in the root folder of the code and added the preceding content to it.

Client app setup to receive notifications

To allow your app to receive notifications in your browser, it will have to get permissions from the user. To do so, we will add a piece of code that will show a consent dialog to let the user grant your app permission to receive notifications in your browser.

We will add the `componentWillMount()` method to our `index.jsx` file present under the home directory, since we want to show the dialog once the user is successfully logged in to the app:

```
componentWillMount() {
    firebase.messaging().requestPermission()
      .then(function() {
        console.log('Permission granted.');
        // you can write logic to get the registration token
```

```
            // _this.getToken();
      })
      .catch(function(err) {
        console.log('Unable to get permission to notify.', err);
      });
  }
```

Note that you will need to import the `firebase` object using the following line:

```
import firebase from '../firebase/firebase-config';
```

Once you add the preceding code, restart your server and log in to the app. It should show the following dialog box to the users of your app:

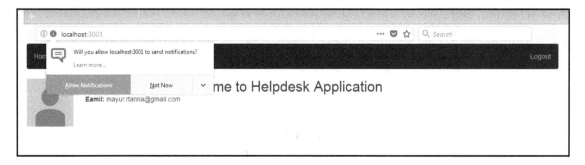

Once user gives permissions then only your browser will receive the notifications.

Now, let's write a function to get the registration token:

```
getToken() {
      console.log("get token");
      firebase.messaging().getToken()
        .then(function (currentToken) {
          if (currentToken) {
            console.log("current token", currentToken)
            // sendTokenToServer(currentToken);
            //updateUI(currentToken);
          } else {
            // Show permission request.
            console.log('No Instance ID token available.
            Request permission to generate one.');
            // Show permission UI.
          // updateUIForPushPermissionRequired();
            // setTokenSentToServer(false);
          }
        })
        .catch(function (err) {
```

```
            console.log('An error occurred while retrieving token.
               ', err);
          // showToken('Error retrieving Instance ID token. ',
               err);
            // setTokenSentToServer(false);
         });
    }
```

The preceding function will retrieve the current access token that will need to be sent to the server to subscribe for the notifications. You can implement logic to send this token to the server in the `sendTokenToServer()` method.

The registration token may change when your web app deletes the registration token or a user clears browser data. In case of the latter, will need to call `getToken()` to retrieve the new token. Since there are chances that the registration token might get changed, you should also monitor refresh token to get the new token. FCM fires a callback whenever a token is generated so that you can get a new token. The `onTokenRefresh()` callback fires whenever a new token is generated, so calling the `getToken()` method in its context ensures that you are having a current registration token. You can write a function like this:

```
refreshToken() {
        firebase.messaging().onTokenRefresh(function () {
            firebase.messaging().getToken()
                .then(function (refreshedToken) {
                    console.log('Token refreshed.');
                    // Indicate that the new Instance ID token has not
                        yet been sent to the
                    // app server.
                    //setTokenSentToServer(false);
                     Send Instance ID token to app server. Implement it
                     as per your requirement
                    //sendTokenToServer(refreshedToken);
                    // ...
                })
                .catch(function (err) {
                    console.log('Unable to retrieve refreshed token ',
                    err);
                    //showToken('Unable to retrieve refreshed token ',
                       err);
                });
        });
    }
```

Once you get the token, you can send it to your app server by implementing a method like `sendTokenToServer(refreshedToken)` to store it and if you are using React and Firebase Realtime Database, you can directly store it in the database.

All these functions will be added to the `index.jsx` file. We will call the `getToken()` function from the `componentWillMount()` method, whereas `refreshToken()` will be called from constructor.

Now, after all this setup, we will add the actual functionality of receiving the messages in our client app.

Depending on the page status, whether it is running in the background or in the foreground (it has focus) or it is closed or hidden behind tabs, the behavior of messages differs.

In order to receive messages, a page must handle the `onMessage()` callback, and to handle `onMessage()`, there must be a Firebase messaging service worker defined in your app.

We will create a file called `firebase-messaging-sw.js` under the root directory of the project and write the following code in it:

```
importScripts('https://www.gstatic.com/firebasejs/4.1.1/firebase-app.js');
importScripts('https://www.gstatic.com/firebasejs/4.1.1/firebase-messaging.js');

var config = {
    messagingSenderId: "41428255555"
};
firebase.initializeApp(config);
const messaging = firebase.messaging();

messaging.setBackgroundMessageHandler(function(payload) {
    console.log('[firebase-messaging-sw.js] Received background message ',
payload);
    // Customize notification here
    const notificationTitle = 'Background Message Title';
    const notificationOptions = {
        body: 'Background Message body.',
        icon: '/firebase-logo.png'
    };

return self.registration.showNotification(notificationTitle,
    notificationOptions);
});
```

Alternatively, you can specify an existing service worker with `useServiceWorker`.

Note that you will need to update the message `senderId` value, which you can get from the Firebase console for your project.

If you want to show a notification message when your web page is in the background, you need to set `setBackgroundMessageHandler` to handle the messages. You can also customize the message, such as setting a custom title and icon. You can check it in the preceding code snippet. The messages received while the app is in the background trigger a display notification in the browser.

Now you can handle the `OnMessage()` event on your web page. We will add a constructor in our `index.js` file so that it registers the callback on page load:

```
constructor(props) {
        super(props);
        //this.refreshToken();
        firebase.messaging().onMessage(function (payload) {
            console.log("Message received. ", payload);
            // Update the UI to include the received message.
            console.log("msg", payload);
            // appendMessage(payload);
        });
    }
```

Now our client is ready to receive the notification messages. Let's configure our backend to send the notifications.

Server setup to send the notifications

The first step is to enable FCM API for your project. You can go to `https://console.developers.google.com/apis/api/fcm.googleapis.com/overview?project=<project-id>` and enable it.

To send the notification from a trusted environment, we will need an Oauth2 access token and the client registration token that we get in the client app.

To get the Oauth2 access token, we will need the private keys from your service account. Once you generate the private key, save the JSON file containing your private key at some secure place. We will use Google API Client Library at `https://developers.google.com/api-client-library/` to retrieve the access token, so install the `npm` module for `googleapis` using the following command:

```
npm install googleapis --save
```

The following function needs to be added to our `main.js` file to get the access token:

```
app.get('/getAccessToken', function (req, res) {

  var { google } = require('googleapis');

  var key = require('./firebase/serviceAccountKey.json');
  var jwtClient = new google.auth.JWT(
    key.client_email,
    null,
    key.private_key,
    ['https://www.googleapis.com/auth/firebase.messaging'], // an array
     of auth scopes
    null
  );
  jwtClient.authorize(function (err, tokens) {
    if (err) {
      console.log(err);
      res.send(JSON.stringify({
        "token": err
      }));
    }
    console.log("tokens", tokens);
    res.send(JSON.stringify({
      "token": tokens.access_token
    }));
  });

});
```

It will show you an access token in your browser when you hit the `http://localhost:3000/getAccessToken` URL.

You will see something like this in your browser:

Obviously, in a real application, you won't show this token in browser or print it in browser console for security reasons, and you will use it internally.

This access token will be passed in the `Authorization` header of the request, as follows:

```
headers: {
  'Authorization': 'Bearer ' + accessToken
}
```

So now you have the access token. Also, if you remember, we talked about the `sendTokenToServer(currentToken)` method when setting up the client app, which sends the token to the server. You must have stored it in your database or cache, which can now be used.

Now we are ready to send our first notification message. To send the message, we will be using the latest HTTP v1 `send` requests.

Our request will look like this:

```
POST https://fcm.googleapis.com/v1/projects/demoproject-7cc0d/messages:send

Content-Type: application/json
Authorization: Bearer
ya29.c.ElphBTDpfvg35hKz4nDu9XYn3p1jlTRgw9FD0ubT5h4prOtwC9G9IKslBv8TDaAPohQH
Y0-O3JmADYfsrk7WWdhZAeOoqWSH4wTsVyijjhE-PWRSL2YI1erT"

{
  "message":{
    "token" :
"dWOV8ukFukY:APA91bFIAEkV-9vwAIQNRGt57XX2hl5trWf8YpocOHfkYAkgSZr5wfBsNozYZO
Em_N0mbdZmKbvmtVCCWovrng4UYwj-
zmpe36ySPcP31HxGGGb3noEkeBFyZRDUpv0TD7HAKxTfDuEx...",
      "notification" : {
        "body" : "This is an FCM notification message!",
        "title" : "FCM Message",
      }
  }
}
```

You will replace all tokens and update the URL with your project ID, and then you should be able to send your first message.

I've used a rest client to send the message and, since my browser is running in background, it shows the notification message in a system tray. You can see that in the next screenshot:

Postman chrome tool extension; the purpose is just to show the request and response of sending the FCM notification message

The request body looks like this:

Postman chrome tool extension; the purpose of the image is just to show the body of the request that we sent earlier

Here are the important things to note about the message request:

URL: `https://fcm.googleapis.com/v1/projects/<projectid>/messages:send`

- Header: contains two key-value pairs:
    - `Content-Type: application/json`
    - `Authorization: Bearer` <access token>
- Request body: Contains the message object with the following key values:
    - `token`: <registration token for the client app to send the message to>
    - `notification`: It contains the configuration for your notiification message

Yeah, so now we have FCM integrated in our app to send the notification message to a single device where an app is running in the background. However, you would want to send the notifications to a group of devices or may want to send the messages to a topic to which clients have subscribed. The basic concept will remain the same, but there will be changes in the configuration. You can refer to those topics in the firebase documentation at `https://firebase.google.com/docs/cloud-messaging`.

We will see Cloud Functions in the next section.

Cloud Functions

Generally, any software application has some kind of backend logic that gets deployed on the server to be accessible through the internet. In case of big enterprise-level applications such as Banking or Finance, it may be worth to manage a server or cluster of servers. However, in case of small applications or the application where you want to execute certain logic depending on some user events, such as data changes in database or on API requests from mobile app or a web application, managing a server may be an overhead in terms of efforts as well as cost. However, when you use the Firebase platform, you don't need to worry about it as it provides **Cloud Functions** that lets you run code based on events emitted by specific Firebase products without managing servers.

Key features of Cloud Functions

Cloud Functions come with a lot features, including easy integration with other Firebase Products and third-party APIs, and powerful security and privacy.

The key features of the Cloud Functions are discussed in the following subtopics.

Seamless integration with other Firebase Products and third-party APIs

Cloud Functions can be seamlessly integrated with other Firebase Products and third-party APIs.

Your custom functions can be executed on specific events, which can be emitted by the listed Firebase products:

- Cloud Firestore Triggers
- Realtime Database Triggers
- Firebase Authentication Triggers
- Google Analytics for Firebase Triggers
- Cloud Storage Triggers
- Cloud Pub/Sub Triggers
- HTTP Triggers

You can use Firebase Admin SDK for seamless integration of across different Firebase products. It is very useful in some of the most common application requirements. Let's say that you want to generate database indexes or audit logs when something changes in your real-time database; you can write a cloud function that is executed based on Realtime database triggers. The other way around, you can do some database operation based on specific user behavior. Similarly, you can integrate Cloud Functions with **Firebase Cloud Messaging** (**FCM**) to notify users when specific events occur in your database.

Cloud Functions integration is not limited to only Firebase products; you can also integrate Cloud Functions with some third-party API services—by writing webhooks. Let's say you are part of a development team and want to update your Slack channel when somebody commits the code to Git. You can use the Git Webhook API, which will trigger your Cloud Function that executes logic to send the message to the Slack Channel. Similarly, you may use third-party Auth provider APIs, such as LinkedIn, to allow user login.

No server to maintain

Cloud Functions run your code without requiring you to purchase or maintain any servers. You can write a Javascript or Typescript function and deploy it with a single command on the cloud. You don't need to worry about server maintenance or scaling. Firebase platform will automatically manage it for you. The scaling of the server instances happens precisely, depending on the workload.

Private and secure

The application business logic should be hidden from client side and must be secure enough to prevent any manipulation or reverse engineering of the code. Cloud Functions is fully secured, so it always remains private and will always do what you want.

Life cycle of a function

Life cycle of a Cloud function can be roughly divided into five stages, which are these:

1. You write code for a new function and define the conditions when the function should get executed. The function definition or code also contains the details of the event provider, such as Realtime database or FCM.
2. You deploy the function using the Firebase CLI, and Firebase connects it to the event provider defined in the code.
3. When the event provider generates the event that matches the conditions defined in the function, it gets executed.
4. Google automatically scales the number of instances based on the workload.
5. Whenever you update the code of a function or delete a function, Google will automatically update or clean up the instances, respectively.

Let's now create a simple Cloud function with Realtime database provider and deploy it.

Setup of Firebase SDK for Cloud Functions

It is necessary to have Firebase CLI installed to proceed further to initialize the Cloud Functions. You can install the Firebase CLI, as given in the next section, if not done already.

Firebase CLI

We have already seen in *Chapter 5*, *User Profile and Access Management*, how to install it but here's the command, just for reference:

```
npm install -g firebase-tools
```

Once we have the Firebase CLI installed, we will log in to the firebase console using this command:

```
firebase login
```

This command will open up a browser URL and will ask you to log in. After a successful login, you can go to the next step—initialization of the Firebase project.

Initializing the Firebase Cloud project

Let's create an empty project directory called cloud-functions. We will run the following command from the newly created cloud -functions directory to initialize the Cloud Functions:

```
firebase init functions
```

This command will walk you through a wizard with different steps and will create the necessary files for your projects. It will ask for your preferred language: Javascript or TypeScript. We will go with the Typescript for this sample. It will also ask you whether you want to associate any existing firebase projects or want to create a new project to associate with it. We will select an existing project. It also asks you if you want it to install the required node dependencies. We will say yes so that it installs all the necessary node packages. If you want to manage the dependencies yourself, you can say no to it. The following screenshot shows how the wizard looks:

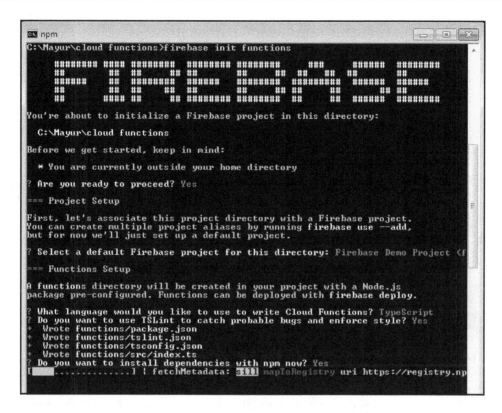

The final structure will look like this:

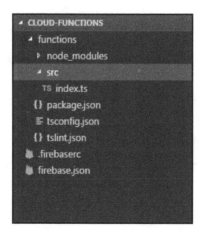

Let's understand some of these files specific to Cloud function:

1. `firebase.json`: It includes properties of your project. It contains a property called "source", which points to the `functions` folder for your Cloud function code. If you want to point to some other folder, you change it here. It also includes a property called "predeploy", which essentially contains the command to build and run your code.

2. `.firebaserc`: It contains projects that are associated with this directory. It helps you quickly switch between projects.

3. `functions/src/index.ts`: This is the main source file where all your Cloud function code will go. By default, a function called `helloworld` will already be there in this file. However, it is commented out by default.

4. `functions/package.json`: Contains NPM dependencies of this project.

If you are a Windows user, you may have to change the value of the property "predeploy" in your `firebase.json` file from "npm --prefix $RESOURCE_DIR run build" to "npm --prefix %RESOURCE_DIR% run build", as it sometimes gives an error when you try to deploy your function.

Once the setup is complete, we are good to go with the deployment of our first cloud function. For this sample, we will write a simple function call `greetUser`, which accepts the name of user in the `request` parameter and show a greeting message in response:

```
import * as functions from 'firebase-functions';

export const greetUser = functions.https.onRequest((request, response) => {
    const name = request.query.name;
    response.send("Welcome to Firebase Cloud Function, "+name+"!");
});
```

First of all, we need to import *firebase-functions* to make our functions work. Also, note that the Cloud Function is implemented by calling `functions.https`, which essentially means that we are using an HTTP trigger.

The `greetUser()` Cloud function is an HTTP endpoint. If you know ExpressJS programming, you must have noted that the syntax resembles ExpressJS endpoint, which executes a function with request and response objects when a user hits the endpoint. Actually, the event handler for an HTTP function listens for the `onRequest()` event, which supports routers and apps managed by the Express web framework. The response object is used to send response back to the user, in our case, a text message, which the user will see in the browser.

Deployment and execution of Cloud Function

We need to use the following command to deploy our `helloworld` Cloud function:

```
firebase deploy --only functions
```

This command will deploy our function, and you should see the following response in your Command Prompt:

```
C:\Windows\System32\cmd.exe
C:\Mayur\react-book\cloud-functions>firebase deploy --only functions

=== Deploying to 'seat-booking'...

i  deploying functions
Running command: npm --prefix %RESOURCE_DIR% run build

> functions@ build C:\Mayur\react-book\cloud-functions\functions
> tsc

+  functions: Finished running predeploy script.
i  functions: ensuring necessary APIs are enabled...
+  functions: all necessary APIs are enabled
i  functions: preparing functions directory for uploading...
i  functions: packaged functions (5.82 KB) for uploading
+  functions: functions folder uploaded successfully
i  functions: updating function greetUser...
+  functions[greetUser]: Successful update operation.
Function URL (greetUser): https://us-central1-seat-booking.cloudfunctions.net/greetUser

+  Deploy complete!

Project Console: https://console.firebase.google.com/project/seat-booking/overview
```

If the deployment has been completed successfully, you will see the function URL, such as `https://us-central1-seat-booking.cloudfunctions.net/greetUser`, which can now be used to trigger the execution of the Cloud Function.

The function URL includes the following:

- `us-central1`: This is the region in which your function is deployed
- `seat-booking`: This is the Firebase project ID
- `cloudfunction.net`: This is the default domain
- `greetUser`: This is the name of the function deployed

We need to append pass name property as a request parameter to see that name in the greeting message.

You should see the following output when you hit that URL from your browser:

So we have successfully created a Cloud function, yay!

Most developers would want to unit test their functions before deploying them on production or test environments. You can deploy and test your functions locally using the following command:

```
firebase serve --only functions
```

It will start a local server and show a URL that you can hit to test your function:

```
C:\Windows\System32\cmd.exe - firebase serve --only functions
C:\Mayur\react-book\cloud-functions>firebase serve --only functions
=== Serving from 'C:\Mayur\react-book\cloud-functions'...
i functions: Preparing to emulate functions.
Warning: You're using Node.js v7.10.0 but Google Cloud Functions only supports v6.11.1.
+ functions: greetUser: http://localhost:5000/seat-booking/us-central1/greetUser
```

In this example, we saw how we can trigger a function through an HTTP request using `functions.https`. Let's explore all Triggering Functions now.

Triggering Functions

Cloud Functions can be executed in response to the events generated by other Firebase products, which are essentially triggers for the Cloud Functions. We have seen the list of all triggers in the Key Features section. We will talk about Realtime Database Triggers, Authentication Triggers, Cloud storage Triggers, and Cloud Firestore Triggers, which are most relevant to this book. The rest three can be explored in the Firebase documentation at https://firebase.google.com/docs/functions/.

Realtime Database Triggers

We can create Cloud Functions, which can respond to Realtime database changes to execute certain tasks. We can create a new function for Realtime Database events with `functions.database`. To specify when the function gets executed, we need to use one of the event handlers that are available to handle different database events. We also need to specify the database path to which the function will listen for events.

Given here are the events that are supported by Cloud Functions:

- `onWrite()` : It triggers when data is created, destroyed, or changed in the Realtime Database
- `onCreate()`: It triggers when new data is created in the Realtime Database

onUpdate(): It triggers when data is updated in the Realtime Database

onDelete(): It triggers when data is deleted from the Realtime Database

We can see the sample Realtime database function, which listens to users path in the database, and, whenever there is any change in the data of any user, it converts the name to uppercase and sets it as a sibling of the user's database. Here, we are using a wildcard `{userId}`, which essentially means any `userId`:

```
import * as functions from 'firebase-functions';
import * as admin from 'firebase-admin';

admin.initializeApp(functions.config().firebase);


export const makeUppercase = functions.database.ref('/users/{userId}')
    .onWrite(event => {
        // Grab the current value of what was written to the Realtime
            Database.
        const original = event.data.val();
        console.log('Uppercasing', original);
        //status is a property
        const uppercase = original.name.toUpperCase();
        // You must return a Promise when performing asynchronous tasks
            inside a Functions such as
        // writing to the Firebase Realtime Database.
        // Setting an "uppercase" sibling in the Realtime Database
            returns a Promise.
        return event.data.ref.parent.child('uppercase').set(uppercase);
});
```

Here, `event.data` is a DeltaSnapshot. iT has a property called 'previous' that lets you check what was saved to the database before the event. The previous property returns a new DeltaSnapshot where all methods refer to the previous value.

Authentication triggers

Using Authentication triggers, we can execute function code in response to the creation and deletion of a user via Firebase Authentication.

To create a Cloud function that is executed if a new user is created, we can use the following code:

```
exports.userCreated = functions.auth.user().onCreate(event => { ... });
```

According to the Firebase documentation, user creation events for Cloud Functions occur in the following scenarios:

- The developer creates an account using the Firebase Admin SDK
- A user creates an email account and password
- A user signs in for the first time using a federated identity provider
- A user signs in to a new anonymous auth session for the first time

A Cloud Functions event is *not* triggered when a user signs in for the first time using a custom token. If you would like to access attributes of a newly created user, you can do so using the `event.data` object.

For example, you can get the user's email and name as follows:

```
const user = event.data;

const email = user.email;
const name = user.displayName;
```

Apart from user creation, if you want to trigger a function on user deletion, you can do it using the `onDelete()` event handler:

```
exports.deleteUser = functions.auth.user().onDelete(event => {
  // ...
});
```

Cloud Storage Triggers

With Cloud Storage Triggers, you can execute a Firebase Cloud Function in response to create, update, or delete operation of files and folders in Cloud Storage. We can create a new function for Cloud Storage events with *functions.storage*. Depending on the requirement, you can have a function that listens for all changes on the default storage bucket, or you can restrict it to a specific bucket by specifying the bucket name:

```
functions.storage.object() - listen for object changes on the default
storage bucket.
functions.storage.bucket('test').object() - listen for object changes on a
specific bucket called 'test'
```

For example, we can write a function that compresses the uploaded files to reduce the size:

```
exports.compressFiles = functions.storage.object().onChange(event => {
  // ...
});
```

The *change* event gets triggered whenever an object is created, modified, or deleted.

The following attributes are exposed by Cloud Storage functions, which can be used to do the further processing of files:

- `event.data`: Represents the storage object.
- `event.data.bucket`: The storage bucket inside which the file is stored.
- `event.data.name`: The file path in the bucket.
- `event.data.contentType`: The file content type.
- `event.data.resourceState`: Two possible values: `exists` or `not_exists`. The `not_exists` value is set if the file / folder has been deleted.
- `event.data.metageneration`: Number of times the metadata of the file has been generated; for new objects, the initial value is `1`.

A most common use case for a Firebase Cloud Function is to further process a file, for example, compress the file or generate thumbnails of an image file.

HTTP Triggers

We have already seen an example of HTTP endpoint called `greetUser()`, which covers most of the essential parts of HTTP endpoints. There's just one important point to note, that we should always terminate our functions properly; else, they might continue to run, and the system will forcibly terminate it. We can end our function with `send()`, `redirect()`, or `end()`.

Consider this example:

```
response.send("Welcome to the Cloud Function");
```

Also, if you are using Firebase hosting and want to connect your HTTP endpoint with some custom domain, you can do that as well.

Cloud Firestore Triggers

Using Cloud Firestore Triggers, your Cloud function can listen to the events emitted by Cloud Firestore whenever there is a change in the data on the specified path your function listens to.

At a high level, it works similarly to the Realtime database triggers. You can use the `functions.firestore` object to listen to the specific events.

It supports four events: create, update, delete, and write, as listed:

- `onWrite()`: It triggers when any document is created, updated, or deleted
- `onCreate()`: It triggers when a new document is created
- `onUpdate()`: It triggers when any value in an existing document is changed
- `onDelete()`: It triggers when a document is deleted

If you want to execute a function whenever a specific document gets changed, you can write a function like this:

```
exports.updateUser = functions.firestore
  .document('users/{userID}')
  .onWrite(event => {
    // An object with the current document value
    var document = event.data.data();

    // An object with the previous document value (for update or
        delete)
    var oldDocument = event.data.previous.data();
```

```
    // perform desited database operations ...
});
```

We will now talk about Cloud function termination.

Function termination

The advantage of the Cloud Functions is that you don't need to procure any servers on your own, so you just need to pay charges for the duration that your Cloud Function runs. This also gives you a responsibility that you terminate your function properly and don't keep your function running in an infinite loop, otherwise it will incur extra charges in your bill.

To terminate your function and manage its life cycle properly, you can follow these recommended approaches:

1. Resolve asynchronous processing functions by returning a JavaScript promise
2. End HTTP functions with `res.redirect()`, `res.send()`, or `res.end()`
3. End a synchronous function with a `return;` statement

Summary

In this chapter, we talked about two advanced features of Firebase: Firebase Cloud Messaging and Firebase Cloud Functions. Using these two features, you can develop a highly interactive serverless app.

FCM is a messaging platform for reliable message delivery of downstream and upstream messages. We also discussed different message types and saw when to use one over another. To have practical experience on FCM, we enhanced our Helpdesk application to send and receive notifications.

We also spoke about Firebase Cloud Functions and saw how it helps to have a serverless app. We covered how to develop a cloud function and deploy it on the server. We also explored the different types of triggers, such as Realtime database triggers, HTTP triggers, Cloud Firestore triggers, Cloud Storage Triggers, and Auth triggers.

In the next chapter, we will cover other advanced and interesting features, such as Firebase Cloud Storage and integration of Firebase application with Google Cloud.

8
Firebase Cloud Storage

In this chapter, we will discuss Cloud Storage for Firebase and also its integration with Google Cloud Platform. We will also explore Firebase hosting, which allows you to host your web apps and static content (CDN) on a production-grade environment.

Cloud Storage provides scalable and secure object storage space, as most of the enterprises today need scalable file storage, considering the huge amount of data they collect through mobile apps, web applications, or corporate websites. Even the applications that are deployed on cloud need storage space either for their own assets such as images, JavaScript, CSS, audio, video files, or user-generated content such as documents, videos, or audios.

The Firebase SDK for Cloud Storage uses Google Cloud Storage buckets to store the uploaded files. Google Cloud Platform needs a billing account to use its products though they provide a few trials. The Firebase SDK for Cloud storage uses a default bucket in Google App Engine free tier and hence you don't need a billing account. Once your app starts growing, you can also integrate other products and services such managed to compute as App Engine or Cloud Functions.

Here's a list of topics that we'll cover in this chapter:

- Overview of Google Cloud Storage
- Key Features of Google Cloud Storage
- Storage Classes supported by Google Cloud Storage
- Overview of Security and **Access Control List** (**ACL**) in Google Cloud Storage
- Key features of Cloud Storage for Firebase
- Setup of the Cloud Storage
- Integrate Firebase Cloud Storage with HelpDesk Application to Upload and Download files
- Overview of Google App Engine
- Overview Firebase Hosting
- Deploy front-end of HelpDesk Application on Firebase Hosting

Before we deep dive into Cloud Storage for Firebase, let's first discuss Google Cloud Storage and its features.

Google Cloud Storage

Google Cloud Platform provides a secure, scalable, cost-effective, and high-performance infrastructure that includes a wide variety of services that are needed for developing, managing, and operating your applications. Google Cloud Storage is a part of Google Cloud Platform, which is a one-stop solution for all your object storage needs—from storage to live streaming to analytics to archival, it covers everything. Object storage is a massively scalable and cost-effective storage service to store any type of data in its native format.

For your different storage requirements, Google Cloud Storage provides different classes of storage, viz, Multi-Regional Storage, Regional Storage, Nearline Storage, and Coldline Storage.

Key features of Google Cloud Storage

Google Cloud Storage delivers advantages in the following key areas:

- **Durable:** Google Cloud Storage is designed to deliver 99.999999999% annual durability. Data is stored redundantly. When you upload data, it gets replicated in the background with an automatic checksum to ensure data integrity.
- **Available:** Google Cloud Storage offers high availability and makes your data available whenever you need it. As per Google Cloud Storage documentation, Multi-Regional offers 99.95% and Regional storage offers 99.9% monthly availability in their Service Level Agreement. Nearline and Coldline storage offer 99% monthly availability.
- **Scalable:** Google Cloud Storage is infinitely scalable, so it can support small to an exabyte-scale system.
- **Consistent:** Google Cloud Storage ensures read-after-write consistency, meaning that if a write succeeds, the latest copy of the document will always be returned for any GET request, globally. This applies to DELETE or PUT of new or overwritten objects.
- **Secure:** Google Cloud Storage is highly secure and has Google grade security to protect your most critical documents, media, and assets. It also provides different Access Control options so that you can control who has access to storage objects and at what level.

- **Easy to Use:** Google Cloud Storage provides simple and easy-to-use APIs and utility tools to work with object storage.

We need to understand a few basic concepts of Google Cloud Storage to use it effectively. So, let's look at them here:

Key concepts

All data in Cloud Storage belongs to a project. A project consists of APIs, a set of users, and security and monitoring settings. You can create as many projects as you want. Inside projects, we have data containers called Buckets, which hold our uploaded data as objects. An object is nothing but a file and optionally, some metadata that describes that file.

Buckets

Buckets are containers that hold your data. They are like directories in the computer file system and are basic containers where you put your data. The only difference is that you can't nest the buckets, unlike directories. Everything that you put in Cloud Storage must be inside a bucket. Buckets allow you to organize your data and also allow you to control access permissions to your data. When designing your application, you should plan fewer buckets and more objects in most cases due to some imposed rate limits of bucket creation and deletion. It is approximately 1 operation every 2 seconds per project.

You need to specify three things when you create a bucket: a globally unique name, a default storage class, and a geographic location where the bucket and its contents are stored. The default storage class you choose applies to the objects inside that bucket if you don't specify an object class explicitly while storing the objects.

Once the bucket is created, you can't change the name of the bucket and its location, unless you delete and recreate it. However, you can change its default storage class to any other class available in the bucket's location.

Bucket names should be globally unique and can be used with CNAME redirect.

Your bucket names must meet the following requirements:

- It must contain only lowercase letters, numbers, and special characters: dashes (-), underscores (_), and dots (.). Names containing dots require verification.
- It must start and end with a number or letter.

- It must be 3 to 63 characters long. Names containing dots can be 222 characters long, but each dot-separated component must not be longer than 63 characters.
- It must not represent an IP address, such as `192.168.1.1`.
- It cannot begin with the "goog" prefix and cannot contain google or misspellings of google.

Apart from names, you can also associate key-value metadata pairs called bucket labels to your buckets. Bucket labels allow you to group your buckets with other Google Cloud Platform services, such as Virtual Machine Instances and Persistent Disks. You can have a maximum of 64 buckets labels per bucket.

Objects

Objects are the basic entities that you store in Cloud Storage. You can store an infinite number of objects in a bucket, so essentially, there is no limit.

Objects consist of *object data* and object metadata. Object data is typically a file and is opaque (a chunk of data) to Cloud storage. Object metadata is a set of key-value pairs that describe the object.

An object name should be unique in a bucket; however, different buckets can have objects with the same name. An object's name is a piece of object metadata in Cloud Storage. Object names can contain any combination of Unicode characters (UTF-8 encoded) and must be less than 1024 bytes in length.

Your object names must meet the following requirements:

- Object names must not contain Carriage Return or Line Feed characters
- Object names must not start with well-known/acme-challenge

You can include a common character slash (/) in your object names if you want to make it appear as though they are stored in a hierarchical structure, for example, /team.

A common character to include in object names is a slash (/). By using slashes, you can make objects appear as though they're stored in a hierarchical structure. For example, you can name one object `/team/alpha/report1.jpg` and another `object/team/alpha/report2.jpg`. They appear to be in a hierarchical directory structure based on the team when you list these objects; however, for Cloud Storage, objects are individual pieces of data and not a hierarchical structure.

Apart from the name, each object has an associated number called **Generation Number**. Whenever your object gets overwritten, its generation number changes. Cloud storage also supports a feature called Object Versioning that allows you to refer to the overwritten or deleted objects. Once you have object versioning enabled for a bucket, it creates an archived version of the object that is overwritten or deleted and associates a unique generation number to uniquely identify an object.

Resources

Any entity within Google Cloud Platform is a resource. Whether it is a project or a bucket or an object, in Google Cloud Platform, it is a resource.

Each resource has an associated unique name that identifies it. Each bucket has a resource name in the form of `projects/_/buckets/`[BUCKET_NAME], where [BUCKET_NAME] is the ID of the bucket. Each object has a resource name in the form of `projects/_/buckets/`[BUCKET_NAME]`/objects/`[OBJECT_NAME], where [OBJECT_NAME] is the ID of the object.

A #[NUMBER] can also be appended to the end of the resource name that indicates a specific generation of the object; #0 is a special identifier to represent the latest version of an object. When the name of the object ends in a string that would otherwise be interpreted as a generation number, #0 can be useful.

Object immutability

In Cloud Storage, when an object is uploaded, you cannot change it throughout its lifetime. The time between successful object upload and successful object delete is an object's lifetime. This essentially means that you cannot modify an existing object by appending some data to it or by truncating some data from it. However, you can overwrite the objects in Cloud storage. Note that the older version of the document will be accessible to the users until successful upload of the new version of the document.

 A single particular object can only be updated or overwritten up to once per second.

So, now that we are aware of the basics of Cloud Storage, let's explore the Storage classes available in Cloud Storage.

Storage classes

Google Cloud Storage supports a range of storage classes based on different use cases. These include Multi Regional and Regional Storage for frequently accessed data, Nearline Storage for less frequently access data, such as data you use not more than once a month, and Coldline storage for infrequently accessed data, such as data you use very rarely, like once a year.

Let's go through them one by one.

Multi regional storage

Multi regional storage is a Geo-redundant storage; it stores your data at multiple Geo locations or data centers across the globe. It stores your data in at least two geographic locations separated by at least 100 miles within the multiregional location of the bucket. It is ideal for low latency high availability application where your application serves the content, such as live streaming of videos, audios, or gaming content, to the users across the globe. Due to data redundancy, it provides high availability. It costs slightly more as compared to other storage classes.

It ensures **99.95% availability SLA**[*]. As your data is saved at multiple places, even in case of natural disasters or any other disruptions, it provides high availability.

The data stored as Multi regional storage can be placed only in multiregional locations, such as the United States, the European Union, or Asia, not specific regional locations such as us-central1 or asia-east1.

Regional storage

Regional storage stores data in a specific regional location, instead of having redundancy distributed over different geo-locations. It is cheaper as compared to Multi regional storage and ensures **99.9% availability SLA**[*].

Regional storage is better suited for storing data in the same regional location of your server instances that use that data. It gives you better performance and in addition, it can reduce network charges.

Nearline storage

There are chances that at some point in time, applications or enterprises use only some of the data frequently out of all the collected data. In that case, Multi regional or Regional storage will not be an ideal choice and will be an expensive option. Cloud storage provides another storage class called Nearline storage that can solve the earlier issue. It is a low-cost, storage service for storing less frequently accessed data. Nearline Storage is a better choice than Multi-Regional Storage or Regional Storage in scenarios where slightly lower availability is required. For example, you do some analytics once a month on the data collected throughout the month. It ensures **99.0% availability SLA**[*].

Nearline Storage is also better suited for data backup, disaster recovery, and archival storage. Note, however, that for data accessed less frequently than once a year, Coldline Storage is the most cost-effective choice, as it offers the lowest storage costs.

Coldline storage

Coldline storage is a very-low-cost, highly-durable storage service for data archiving and disaster recovery. Though it is like a "cold storage", it provides low latency access to your data. It is the best choice for data that you need once or twice a year. You can also store your daily backups and archived files to Coldline, as you don't need them on regular basis and will need them only in case of disaster recovery. It ensures **99.0% availability SLA** *.

Standard storage

When users don't specify the default storage class while creating a bucket, it will be considered as a Standard storage object. Objects created without a storage class in such a bucket are also listed as Standard Storage. If the bucket is located in a multiregional location, Standard storage is equivalent to Multi-Regional Storage and when the bucket is in a regional storage, it is considered to be in Regional storage.

Note that pricing will also happen accordingly. If it is equivalent to Multi regional storage, charges of Multi Regional storage will apply.

Now that we know about the different storage classes, let's understand the Life Cycle Management of an object in Cloud Storage.

Life Cycle Management

Many applications require the functionality to delete or archive the older resources after a certain amount of time. The following are some example use cases:

1. Move files older than 1 year from Multi Regional Storage to Coldline Storage.
2. Delete files older than 5 years from Coldline storage.
3. Keep only a few recent object versions if you have Object Versioning.

Luckily, Google Cloud Storage provides a functionality called Object Life Cycle Management to handle this type of operations automatically based on the configurations. The configurations are set of rules that apply to bucket where you have enabled this feature.

For example, the following rule specifies that it delete the files older than 365 days:

```
// lifecycle.json
{
  "lifecycle": {
    "rule":
    [
      {
        "action": {"type": "Delete"},
        "condition": {"age": 365}
      }
    ]
  }
}
```

APIs and tools

Google Cloud Platform provides SDKs for Cloud storage and also a number of other products for a different platform such as Node.js, Java, Python, Ruby, PHP, and go. It provides REST APIs if you are not using any client library. It also provides a command-line tool called **gsutil** that allows you to perform object management tasks, including the following:

- Upload, download, and delete objects
- List buckets and objects
- Move, Copy, and rename objects
- Edit object and bucket ACLs

Access control

There are a number of options available for access management of your buckets and objects. Let's see a summary:

1. **Identity and Access Management (IAM)** permissions: Gives broad level control for your projects and buckets. It is useful to grant access to buckets and allow bulk operations on objects within a bucket.
2. **Access Control Lists (ACLs)**: Gives you fine-grained control to grant read or write access to users to individual buckets or objects.
3. Signed URLs (query string authentication): Grant read or write access to an object for a limited time period through a Signed URL.
4. **Signed Policy Documents**: Allows you to define rules and perform validations for what objects can be uploaded in a bucket, for example, restrict based on file size or content-type.
5. **Firebase Security Rules**: Provides granular and attribute-based rule language to provide access to mobile apps and web apps using the Firebase SDKs for Cloud Storage.

Now that we are familiar with the key concepts of Google Cloud Storage, let's come back to Cloud Storage for Firebase.

Key features of Cloud Storage for Firebase

Cloud Storage for Firebase inherits advantages or features from Google Cloud Storage. However, it has some additional features, such as declarative security rule language, to specify security rules.

The key features of Cloud Storage are as follows:

1. **Ease of use and Robustness**: Cloud storage for Firebase is a simple and powerful solution to store and retrieve the user-generated content such as documents, photos, audio, or videos. It provides robust upload and download capabilities so that file transfers get paused when internet connectivity drops and resume from where they were left when it is connected again. It saves time as well as your internet bandwidth. The API for Cloud storage is also easy and can be used through the use of Firebase SDK.

2. **Powerful Security:** When it comes to storage in the cloud, the first thing we think about is the security. Is it secure enough? What will happen to my documents? Such questions are obvious and important also. The answer to that is yes, Cloud storage for Firebase is very much secure. It has the power of Google security. It is integrated with Firebase authentication to provide intuitive authentication for developers. You can also use declarative security rules to restrict access to the files based on the content type, name, or some other attributes.

3. **High Scalability:** Cloud storage for Firebase is backed by Google infrastructure, which provides a highly scalable storage environment so that you can easily scale your applications from prototypes to productions. This infrastructure already backs the most popular and high traffic applications, such as Youtube, Google photos, and Spotify.

4. **Cost effective:** Cloud storage is a cost-effective solution where you just pay for what you use. You don't need to purchase and maintain a server for hosting files.

5. **Integrates well with other Firebase products:** Cloud storage integrates well with other Firebase products, for example, in our last chapter, we have seen that Cloud storage triggers can trigger the Cloud functions that can execute some logic based on the file operation on Cloud storage.

We have seen the key features and advantages of Cloud Storage for Firebase. Let's see how it actually works.

How does it work?

Firebase SDKs for Cloud Storage can be used to upload and download files directly from clients. The client is able to retry to resume the operation right where it left off, saving your user's time and bandwidth.

Under the hood, Cloud Storage stores your files in a Google Cloud Storage bucket and hence makes them accessible through both Firebase and Google Cloud. This gives you the flexibility to upload and download files from mobile clients via the Firebase SDKs, and do server-side processing, such as image thumbnail generation or video transcoding using Google Cloud Platform. As we have seen that Cloud Storage scales automatically, it can handle all types of application data, small to medium to large applications.

On the security front, the Firebase SDKs for Cloud Storage integrate seamlessly with Firebase Authentication to identify users. As we saw in `Chapter 6`, *Firebase Security and Rules*, Firebase also provides declarative rule language that lets you control access to individual files or groups of files.

Let's enhance our Helpdesk application where the user can upload their profile picture.

Setting up the Cloud Storage

With Firebase SDK, we can easily integrate and set up Cloud Storage for Firebase in our application.

To set up Cloud Storage, you will need the URL of the Storage bucket, which you can get from our Firebase Console. You can get it from the `Files` tab of `Storage` menu, as illustrated:

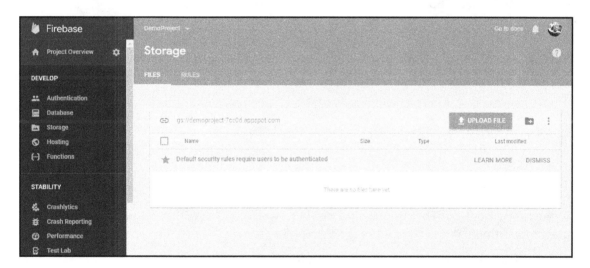

Once you get it, you can add it to your Firebase config.

Consider this example:

```
import firebase from 'firebase';

const config = {
    apiKey: "AIzaSyDO1VEnd5VmWd2OWQ9NQkkkkh-ehNXcoPTy-w",
    authDomain: "demoproject-7cc0d.firebaseapp.com",
    databaseURL: "https://demoproject-7cc0d.firebaseio.com",
```

```
        projectId: "demoproject-7cc0d",
        storageBucket: "gs://demoproject-7cc0d.appspot.com",
        messagingSenderId: "41428255555"
    };

    export const firebaseApp = firebase.initializeApp(config);

    // Get a reference to the storage service,
    var storage = firebase.storage();
```

Now we are ready to use Cloud storage. Now we need to create a reference, which can be used to navigate through the file hierarchy.

We can get a reference by calling a `ref()` method, like this:

```
    var storage = firebase.storage();
```

You can also create a reference to a specific lower node in a tree. For example, to get a reference to `images/homepage.png`, we can write something like this:

```
    var homepageRef = storageRef.child('images/homepage.jpg');
```

You can also navigate to upper or lower level in a file hierarchy:

```
    // move to the parent of a reference - refers to images
    var imagesRef = homepageRef.parent;

    //move to highest parent or top of the bucket
    var rootRef = homepageRef.root;

    //chaining can be done for root, parent and child for multiple times
    homepageRef.parent.child('test.jpg');
```

Three properties—**fullPath**, **name**, and **bucket**—are available with references to better understand the files that references are a point to:

```
    // File path is 'images/homepage.jpg'
    var path = homepageRef.fullPath

    // File name is 'homepage.jpg'
    var name = homepageRef.name

    // Points to 'images'
    var imagesRef = homepageRef.parent;
```

Now we are ready for the upload functionality. We will extend our HelpDesk application and give the user a functionality to upload the screenshot along with other details of the ticket. We will store the uploaded picture in Cloud storage for Firebase and retrieve it from there only.

Upload Files

You can upload File or Blob types, a Uint8Array or base64 encoded strings to upload files to Cloud Storage. For our example, we will use File type. As mentioned earlier, first we need to get a reference to the full path of the file, including the filename.

We will modify the AddTicketForm.jsx file to allow the user to upload a screenshot or an image related to the ticket.

The src/add-ticket/'AddTicketForm.jsx' file now looks like the following. The changes are highlighted in bold with comments:

```jsx
import React, { Component } from 'react';
import firebase from '../firebase/firebase-config';
import { ToastSuccess, ToastDanger } from 'react-toastr-basic';

class AddTicketForm extends Component {

  constructor(props) {
    super(props);
    this.handleSubmitEvent = this.handleSubmitEvent.bind(this);
    this.handleChange = this.handleChange.bind(this);
    this.onChange = this.onChange.bind(this);
    console.log(props.userInfo);

    this.state = {
      uId: props.userId,
      email: props.userInfo[0].email,
      issueType: "",
      department: "",
      comment: "",
      snapshot: null
    }
  }

  handleChange(event) {
    console.log(event.target.value);
    this.setState({
      [event.target.id]: event.target.value
    });
```

```
    }

    //handle onchange - set the snapshot value to the file selected
    onChange(e) {
      console.log("ff ",e.target.files[0] );
      this.setState({snapshot:e.target.files[0]})
    }

    handleSubmitEvent(e) {
      e.preventDefault();
      var storageRef = firebase.storage().ref();

      // Create a reference to 'image'
      var snapshotRef =
storageRef.child('ticket_snapshots/'+this.state.snapshot.name);
      //get a reference to 'this' in a variable since in callback this will
point to different object
      var _this = this;
      snapshotRef.put(this.state.snapshot).then(function(res) {
        console.log('Uploaded a blob or file!');
        console.log(res.metadata);

        const userId = _this.state.uId;
        var data = {
          date: Date(),
          email: _this.state.email,
          issueType: _this.state.issueType,
          department: _this.state.department,
          comments: _this.state.comment,
          status: "progress",
          snapshotURL: res.metadata.downloadURLs[0]   //save url in db to use
it for download
        }

        console.log(data);


      var newTicketKey =
firebase.database().ref('/helpdesk').child('tickets').push().key;
        // Write the new ticket data simultaneously in the tickets list and
the user's ticket list.
        var updates = {};
        updates['/helpdesk/tickets/' + userId + '/' + newTicketKey] = data;
        updates['/helpdesk/tickets/all/' + newTicketKey] = data;

        return firebase.database().ref().update(updates).then(() => {
          ToastSuccess("Saved Successfully!!");
          this.setState({
```

```
          issueType: "",
          department: "",
          comment: "",
          snapshot: _this.state.snapshot
        });
      }).catch((error) => {
        ToastDanger(error.message);
      });

    });

    //React form data object

  }
  //render() method - snippet given below
  }
export default AddTicketForm;
```

Let's understand the preceding code:

1. Add a snapshot property in the state.
2. OnChange() - register the onChange() event for the file to set it in snapshot field in the state.
3. onHandleSubmit() - We have created a reference to the file to store it in a folder called 'ticket_snapshots' in Firebase Cloud storage. Once the file is uploaded successfully, we will get a download URL from response metadata, which we are storing in our realtime database along with other ticket details.

You will also do some HTML changes in the render() method to add input field for file selection:

```
render() {
  var style = { color: "#ffaaaa" };
  return (
    <form onSubmit={this.handleSubmitEvent} >
      <div className="form-group">
        <label htmlFor="email">Email <span style={style}>*</span></label>
        <input type="text" id="email" className="form-control"
          placeholder="Enter email" value={this.state.email} disabled
          required onChange={this.handleChange} />
      </div>
      <div className="form-group">
        <label htmlFor="issueType">Issue Type <span style={style}>
*</span></label>
        <select className="form-control" value={this.state.issueType}
          id="issueType" required onChange={this.handleChange}>
```

```
            <option value="">Select</option>
            <option value="Access Related Issue">Access Related
            Issue</option>
            <option value="Email Related Issues">Email Related
             Issues</option>
            <option value="Hardware Request">Hardware Request</option>
            <option value="Health & Safety">Health & Safety</option>
            <option value="Network">Network</option>
            <option value="Intranet">Intranet</option>
            <option value="Other">Other</option>
          </select>
        </div>
        <div className="form-group">
          <label htmlFor="department">Assign Department
        <span style={style}> *</span></label>
          <select className="form-control" value={this.state.department}
  id="department" required onChange={this.handleChange}>
            <option value="">Select</option>
            <option value="Admin">Admin</option>
            <option value="HR">HR</option>
            <option value="IT">IT</option>
            <option value="Development">Development</option>
          </select>
        </div>
        <div className="form-group">
          <label htmlFor="comments">Comments <span style={style}>
*</span></label>
          (<span id="maxlength"> 200 </span> characters left)
            <textarea className="form-control" rows="3" id="comment"
value={this.state.comment} onChange={this.handleChange}
required></textarea>
        </div>
        <div className="form-group">
          <label htmlFor="fileUpload">Snapshot</label>
          <input id="snapshot" type="file" onChange={this.onChange} />
        </div>
        <div className="btn-group">
          <button type="submit" className="btn btn-
          primary">Submit</button>
          <button type="reset" className="btn btn-
          default">cancel</button>
        </div>
      </form>
    );
  }
```

Our add-ticket form looks like this:

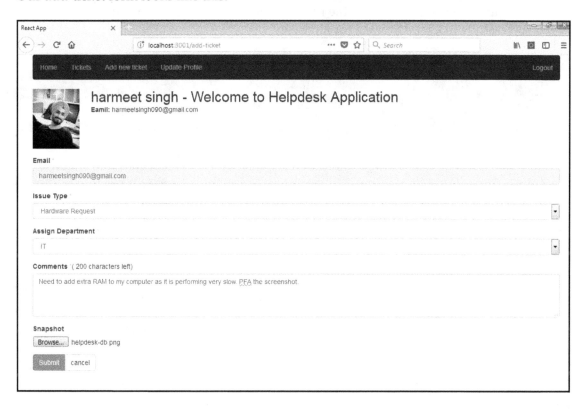

You can then check your Firebase console to see whether file uploading is working or not. The following screenshot shows that the file (`helpdesk-db.png`) we have uploaded is saved successfully in Cloud Storage for Firebase:

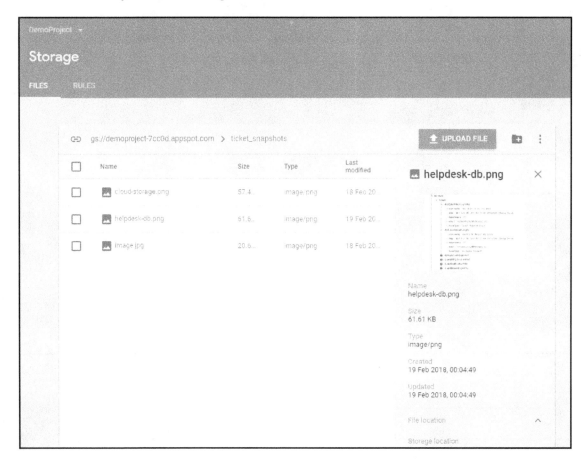

As mentioned earlier, Cloud storage for Firebase is highly integrated with Google Cloud Storage and uses a bucket of Google Cloud Storage to store the files. You can log in to your console of Google Cloud Platform at `https://console.cloud.google.com/storage` and check under the storage section. You should see all your uploaded files there also.

The next screenshot shows that the files can be viewed from Google Cloud Platform console:

Now, you can check your database also to see whether the ticket that has been created has snapshot URL property and corresponding value—downloadURL of the file.

The following screenshot of the database shows that the snapshot URL is getting stored correctly:

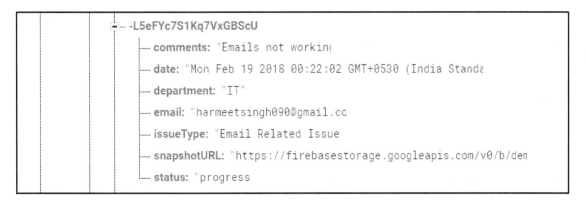

Yay! The Cloud Storage is integrated with our application. However, we are not done yet. We will need to allow the user to see the uploaded images, so we will implement a download file functionality too. However, before we move to download file function, I would like to mention that you should update the security rules for Cloud Storage to control access to your files. As per default rules, Firebase Authentication is required in order to perform any `.read` and `.write` operations on all files.

The default rules look like the following image:

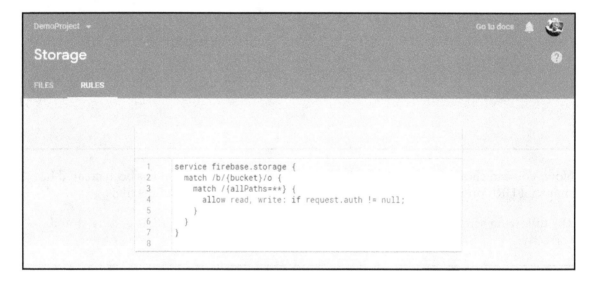

However, you should update them as per your requirement.

Adding file metadata

When you upload a file, you can also store some metadata for that file, such as Content-Type or name.

You can create a JSON object with key: value pairs and pass that object when you upload the file. For custom metadata, you can create an object inside the metadata object, as shown here:

```
// Create file metadata including the content type
var metadata = {
  contentType: 'image/jpeg',
  customMetadata: {
      'ticketNo':'12345'
```

```
    }
};
```

```
// Upload the file and metadata
var uploadTask = storageRef.child('folder/file.jpg').put(file, metadata);
```

Managing uploads and error handling

Cloud Storage allows you to manage the file uploads; you can resume, pause, or cancel the upload. The corresponding methods are available on `UploadTask`, which is returned by the `put()` or `putString()` methods that can be used as a promise or use to manage and monitor the status of the upload:

```
// Upload the file and metadata
var uploadTask = storageRef.child('folder/file.jpg').put(file);

// Pause the upload - state changes to pause
uploadTask.pause();

// Resume the upload - state changes to running
uploadTask.resume();

// Cancel the upload - returns an error indicating file upload is cancelled
uploadTask.cancel();
```

You can use the 'state_change' observer to listen to the progress events. It is very useful if you want to show some real-time progress bar for your file uploading:

Event Type	Usage
running	When the task starts or resumes uploading, this event gets fired.
progress	When any data is uploaded to Cloud Storage, this event gets fired. Useful to show progress bar for upload.
pause	When the upload is paused, this event gets fired.

When an event occurs, a **TaskSnapshot** object will be passed back, which can be used to view the task at the time of event occurrence.

The object is passed back. It contains the following properties:

Property	Type	Description
bytes transferred	`Number`	Total number of bytes that have been transferred when the snapshot was taken.
totalBytes	`Number`	Total number of bytes to be uploaded.
state	`firebase.storage.TaskState`	Current upload state
metadata	`firebaseStorage.Metadata`	Contains metadata sent by server on completion of upload; until then, contains the metadata sent to the server.
task	`firebaseStorage.UploadTask`	Can be used to pause, cancel, or resume the task.
ref	`firebaseStorage.Reference`	The reference this task came from.

When you upload a file, there are chances that some error occurs. You can handle the error using the error object you get in callback.

The following code snippet shows example code to manage the file upload and error handling:

```
// File
var file = this.state.snapshot;

// Create the file metadata
var metadata = {
  contentType: 'image/jpeg'
};

// Upload file and metadata to the object 'images/mountains.jpg'
var uploadTask = storageRef.child('ticket_snapshots/' +
file.name).put(file, metadata);

// Listen for state changes, errors, and completion of the upload.
uploadTask.on(firebase.storage.TaskEvent.STATE_CHANGED, // or
'state_changed'
  function(snapshot) {
    // Get task progress, including the number of bytes uploaded and the
total number of bytes to be uploaded
    var progress = (snapshot.bytesTransferred / snapshot.totalBytes) * 100;
    console.log('Upload is ' + progress + '% done');
```

```
    switch (snapshot.state) {
      case firebase.storage.TaskState.PAUSED: // or 'paused'
        console.log('Upload is paused');
        break;
      case firebase.storage.TaskState.RUNNING: // or 'running'
        console.log('Upload is running');
        break;
    }
  }, function(error) {

    // A full list of error codes is available at
    // https://firebase.google.com/docs/storage/web/handle-errors
    switch (error.code) {
      case 'storage/unauthorized':
        // User doesn't have permission to access the object
        break;

      case 'storage/canceled':
        // User canceled the upload
        break;

      case 'storage/unknown':
        // Unknown error occurred, inspect error.serverResponse
        break;
    }
  }, function() {
    // Upload completed successfully, now we can get the download URL
    var downloadURL = uploadTask.snapshot.downloadURL;
  });
```

Now, let's move to the download file section.

Downloading files

To download a file, you will need to get a reference to that file using either `https://` or `gs://` URL of the file, or you can construct it by appending child paths to the storage root.

The next code snippet shows these methods:

```
var storage = firebase.storage();
var pathReference = storage.ref('images/stars.jpg');

// Create a reference from a Google Cloud Storage URI
var gsReference = storage.refFromURL('gs://bucket/folder/file.jpg')

// Create a reference from an HTTPS URL
```

```
// Note that in the URL, characters are URL escaped!
var httpsReference =
storage.refFromURL('https://firebasestorage..../file.jpg')
```

We will extend our HelpDesk application to allow the user to view the snapshot for a ticket if uploaded any. You will need to update code in the `ViewTickets.jsx` file under the `ticket-listing` folder. We already get a URL from our database, so we don't need to get a reference to get the download URL:

```
componentDidMount() {
    const itemsRef =
firebase.database().ref('/helpdesk/tickets/'+this.props.userId);

    itemsRef.on('value', (snapshot) => {
      let tickets = snapshot.val();
      if(tickets != null){
        let ticketKeys = Object.keys(tickets);
        let newState = [];
        for (let ticket in tickets) {
          newState.push({
            id:ticketKeys,
            email:tickets[ticket].email,
            issueType:tickets[ticket].issueType,
            department:tickets[ticket].department,
            comments:tickets[ticket].comments,
            status:tickets[ticket].status,
            date:tickets[ticket].date,
            snapshotURL: tickets[ticket].snapshotURL
        });
      }
        this.setState({
          tickets: newState
        });
      }
    });
}

render() {
    return (
        <table className="table">
        <thead>
        <tr>
            <th>Email</th>
            <th>Issue Type</th>
            <th>Department</th>
            <th>Comments</th>
            <th>Status</th>
```

```
            <th>Date</th>
            <th>Snapshot</th>
        </tr>
        </thead>
        <tbody>
            {
                this.state.tickets.length > 0 ?
                this.state.tickets.map((item,index) => {
                return (
                    <tr key={item.id[index]}>
                        <td>{item.email}</td>
                        <td>{item.issueType}</td>
                        <td>{item.department}</td>
                        <td>{item.comments}</td>
                        <td>{item.status === 'progress'?'In Progress':''}</td>
                        <td>{item.date}</td>
                        <th><a target="_blank"
href={item.snapshotURL}>View</a></th>
                    </tr>
                )
            }) :
                <tr>
                    <td colSpan="5" className="text-center">No tickets
found.</td>
                </tr>
            }
        </tbody>
        </table>
    );
```

Like for file upload, you need to handle errors for download in a similar manner as well.

Now, let's see how we can delete files from Cloud Storage.

Deleting files

To delete a file, you first need to get a reference to the file, the same as we saw in upload and download. Once you get a reference, you can call a `delete()` method on it to delete a file. It returns a promise that either resolves in case of success or rejects in case of an error.

Consider this example:

```
// Create a reference to the file to delete
var fileRef = storageRef.child('folder/file.jpg');

// Delete the file
```

```
desertRef.delete().then(function() {
  // File deleted successfully
}).catch(function(error) {
  // an error occurred!
});
```

Now, let's see what is Google App Engine.

Google App Engine

Google App Engine is a "Platform as a Service" that abstracts away the infrastructure worries and lets you focus only on code. It provides an automatically scalable platform that scales based on the amount of traffic it receives. You just need to upload your code, and it will automatically manage the availability of your app. Google App Engine is an easy and fast way to add additional processing power or trusted execution to your Firebase application.

If you have an App Engine application, you can use the built-in App Engine APIs to share data between Firebase and App Engine, since the Firebase SDKs for Cloud Storage use the Google App Engine default bucket. This is useful for performing computation intensive background processing or image operations, such as creating a thumbnail of uploaded image.

The Google App Engine standard environment provides an environment where your application runs in a sandbox, using the runtime environment of a supported language viz, Python 2.7, Java 8, Java 7, PHP 5.5, and Go 1.8, 1.6. If you have application code that needs some other version of these languages or needs some another language, you can use the Google App Engine flexible environment where your application runs on docker containers, which run on Google Cloud Virtual machines.

There are many differences between these two environments, which can be explored in the Google Cloud documentation at `https://cloud.google.com/appengine/docs/the-appengine-environments`.

If you want to import an existing Google Cloud Platform project into Firebase and want to make available any existing App Engine objects, you'll need to set the default access control on your objects to allow Firebase to access them by running the following command using `gsutil`:

```
gsutil -m acl ch -r -u firebase-storage@system.gserviceaccount.com:O
gs://<your-cloud-storage-bucket>
```

Firebase hosting

Firebase hosting provides a secure and easy way to host your static website and resources on CDN. The key features of Hosting are as follows:

1. **Served over a secure connection**: Content is always delivered securely over SSL
2. Faster Content Delivery: Files are cached at CDN edges around the globe, so there's faster content delivery.
3. Faster Deployment: You can deploy your app using Firebase CLI within a few seconds
4. Easy and Fast rollback: In case of any mistake, roll back with a single command

Hosting provides all the necessary infrastructure, features, and tooling tailored to deploying and managing static websites, whether it is a single page app or a complex progressive app.

Your site will be hosted on a subdomain on the `firebaseapp.com` domain by default. Using the Firebase CLI, you can deploy files from local directories on your computer to your Hosting server.

When you move your site to production, you can connect your own domain name to Firebase Hosting.

Deploying your site

You will need to install the Firebase CLI to deploy your static web app.

The Firebase CLI can be installed with a single command:

```
npm install -g firebase-tools
```

Now, let's deploy our HelpDesk application on cloud. We have two projects for HelpDesk: react app (a project called code) and server app (a project called node). Let's first host or deploy our client-side react app on Firebase Hosting.

Go inside your project directory (code) and run the following command to initialize the configurations:

```
firebase init
```

As shown in the following screenshot, it will ask you "which Firebase feature do you want to set up for this folder?," and you need to select 'Hosting':

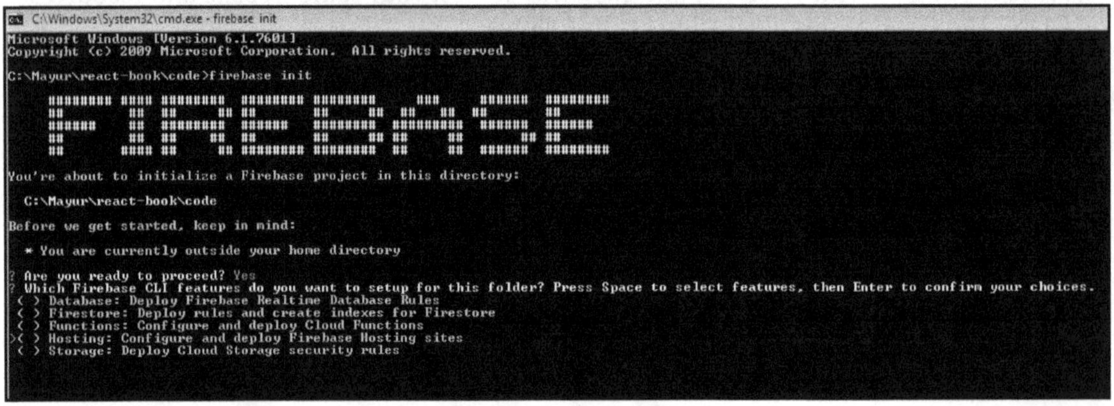

It will create a `firebase.json` file in the root directory of your project. The structure of the `firebase.json` will look like this:

```
{
  "database": {
    "rules": "database.rules.json"
  },
  "hosting": {
    "public": "build",
    "ignore": [
      "firebase.json",
      "**/.*",
      "**/node_modules/**"
    ],
    "rewrites": [
      {
        "source": "**",
        "destination": "/index.html"
      }
    ]
  }
}
```

The public property tells Firebase which directory is to be uploaded to hosting. The directory must exist in your project directory.

You can now deploy your site using the following command:

```
firebase deploy
```

It will ask you to do Firebase CLI login. You can do it using the following command:

```
firebase login --reauth
```

After a successful login, you can run the `firebase deploy` command again to deploy your app:

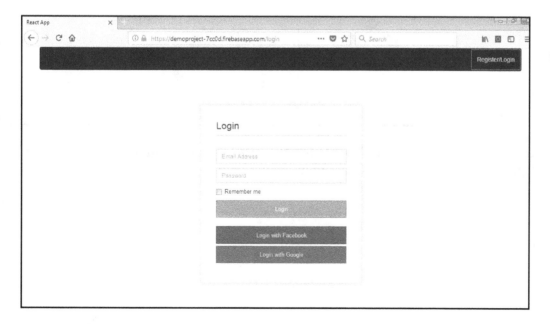

After successful deployment, you will a Hosting URL of your project, which is like `https://YOUR-FIREBASE-APP>.firebaseapp.com`. In our case, it is `https://demoproject-7cc0d.firebaseapp.com/`. *60.* Now you can go and hit the generated URL and confirm that it is accessible:

Yay! We have deployed our first app on Firebase Hosting. You can also check the URL in your Firebase console under **Hosting** section:

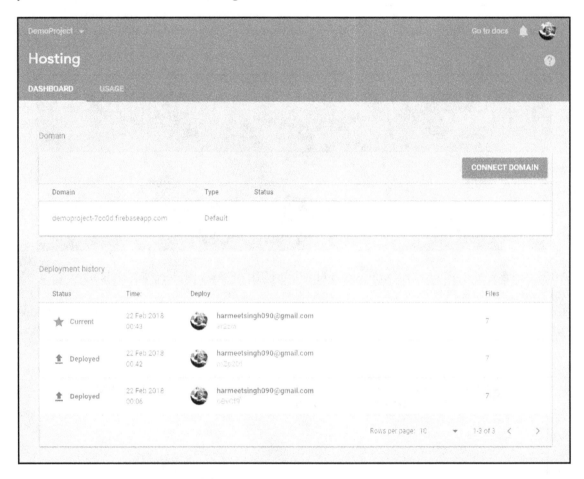

You can also configure your custom domain by clicking on the **Connect Domain** button. It will guide you through a wizard to configure your own domain.

Summary

This chapter introduced the Google Cloud Platform. It gave you a basic understanding of Google Cloud Storage and Google App Engine and how we can integrate Cloud storage for Firebase with Google Cloud Storage. We explored Cloud Storage for Firebase and saw how you can upload, download, and delete files to Cloud Storage. We also extended the HelpDesk application to allow the user to upload a screenshot along with the ticket details and also view/download the uploaded image. In addition, we explored how we can deploy our app on Firebase Hosting.

In the next chapter, we will talk about coding standards and best practices that developers should follow while working with React and Firebase to have better application performance, reduced number of bugs, and also for easily manageable application code.

9
Best Practices

Before diving deep into the best practices to be followed while dealing with React and Firebase, let's recap what we have seen so far in the previous chapters.

In the previous chapters, we saw Firebase account Setup, Firebase integration with ReactJs, Login Authentication With Firebase Auth Providers, Auth State management in React Component, Securing Data based on Role and Profile, Firebase integration with React-Redux, Firebase Cloud Messaging, Firebase Cloud Functions, and Using Firebase Admin SDK API with React Components, and I hope you have also enjoyed this journey. Now we know from where can we start and how to write the code, but the most important stuff is how can we write standard coding by following best practices.

So when we create an application with React and Firebase, we need to ensure that the structure of your data in Firebase Database and passing the data into the react components is the most important part of the application.

In the development field, each developer has an individual opinion for following best practices, but I'm sharing with you what I have observed and experienced so far; you might have a different opinion.

Here's a list of topics that we'll cover in this chapter:

- Best practices with Firebase
- Best practices with React and Redux

Best practices with Firebase

In Firebase, we all know that data is stored in JSON tree format, which is synchronized in realtime to every connected device. So while building cross-platform applications (web, iOS, and Android) with Firebase, we can share one instance to all your apps to receive the latest updates with new data from Realtime Database. So when we add the data into the JSON tree, it becomes the node in the existing JSON Structure with an associated key, so we always need to plan how data will be saved to build a properly structured database.

Writing the data

In Firebase, we have four methods available to write a data into the Firebase database:

`set( )`	**Write or replace data to a defined path, like** `messages/tickets/<uid>`.
`update( )`	Update to specific children of node without replacing the other child nodes. We can also use the update method to update the data into multiple locations.
`push( )`	To add a list of data in the database, we can use the `push()` method; it generates a unique ID every time when it calls, such as `helpdesk/tickets/<unique-user-id>/<unique-ticket-id>`.
`transaction( )`	We can use this method when we are working with complex data that can be corrupted by concurrent updates such as incremental counters.

Now, let's take a look at how data is structured in our helpdesk application:

```
{
  "tickets": {
  "-L4L1BLYiU-UQdE61KA_": {
    "comments": "Need extra 4GB RAM in my system"
    "date": "Fri Feb 02 2018 15:51:10 GMT+0530 (India Standa..."
    "department": "IT"
    "email": "harmeet_15_1991@yahoo.com"
    "issueType": "Hardware Request"
    "status": "progress"
  },
  "-L4K01hUSDzPXTIXY9oU": {
    "comments": "Need extra 4GB RAM in my system"
    "date": "Fri Feb 02 2018 15:51:10 GMT+0530 (India Standa..."
    "department": "IT"
    "email": "harmeet_15_1991@yahoo.com"
    "issueType": "Hardware Request"
```

```
    "status": "progress"
      }
    }
  }
```

Now, let's take an example of the preceding data structure and use the `set()` method to store the data with autoincrementing integer:

```
{
  "tickets": {
  "0": {
      "comments": "Need extra 4GB RAM in my system"
      "date": "Fri Feb 02 2018 15:51:10 GMT+0530 (India Standa..."
      "department": "IT"
      "email": "harmeet_15_1991@yahoo.com"
      "issueType": "Hardware Request"
      "status": "progress"
    },
    "1": {
      "comments": "Need extra 4GB RAM in my system"
      "date": "Fri Feb 02 2018 15:51:10 GMT+0530 (India Standa..."
      "department": "IT"
      "email": "harmeet_15_1991@yahoo.com"
      "issueType": "Hardware Request"
      "status": "progress"
      }
    }
  }
```

Now if you see the preceding data structure, new tickets will be stored as /tickets/1. This will work if only a single user were adding tickets, but in our application, many users can add tickets at the same time. If two employees write to /tickets/2 simultaneously, then one of the tickets will be deleted by the other. So this will not be recommended practices and always recommend to use the push() method to generate a unique ID (refer to the preceding data structure) when you are working with list of data.

Avoid nesting data

In Firebase Realtime Database, when you fetch the data from the JSON tree, we will also get all the child nodes of that specific node, because when we add the data into the JSON tree, it becomes the node in the existing JSON structure with an associated key. Firebase Realtime Database allows nesting data up to 32 levels deep, so when we give the access to someone to read or write access at a specific node, then we are also giving access of all the child nodes of under that node. Therefore, always the best practice is to keep our data structure as flat as possible.

Let me show you why nested data is bad; refer to the following example:

```
{
  // a poorly nested data architecture, because
  // iterating over "products" to get a list of names requires
  // potentially downloading hundreds of products of mobile
  "products": {
  "electronics": {
  "name": "mobile",
  "types": {
  "samsung": { "name": "Samsung S7 Edge (Black Pearl, 128 GB)",
"description": "foo" },
  "apple": { ... },
  // a very long list of mobile products
  }
  }
  }
  }
```

With this nested data structure, it's very difficult to iterate over the data. Even a simple operation like listing the names of products requires that the entire products tree, including all product list and types, be downloaded to the client.

Flattern data structure

In Flattern structure, data was split into different paths; it could be easy to download only the required nodes, as needed:

```
{
        // products contains only meta info about each product
        // stored under the product's unique ID
        "products": {
          "electronics": {
            "name": "mobile"
          },
```

```
        "home_furniture": { ... },
        "sports": { ... }
    },
    // product types are easily accessible (or restricted)
    // we also store these by product Id
    "types": {
        "mobile":{
            "name":"samsung"
        },
    "laptop": {...},
    "computers":{...},
    "television":{...}
    "home_furniture": { ... },
    "sports": { ... }
    },
    // details are separate from data we may want to iterate quickly
    // but still easily paginated and queried, and organized by
        product ID
    "detail": {
      "electronics": {
        "samsung": { "name": "Samsung S7 Edge (Black Pearl, 128 GB)",
        "description": "foo" },
        "apple": { ... },
        "mi": { ... }
      },
      "home_furniture": { ... },
      "sports": { ... }
    }
}
```

In the preceding example, we had some lightly nested data (for example, details for each products are themselves objects with children), but we've also organized our data logically by how it will be iterated and read later. We have stored duplicate data to defining the relationship between objects; this is necessary to maintain the two-way, many-to-many, or one-to-many relationships for redundancy. It allows us to quickly and efficiently fetch mobiles, even when the list of products or products types scales into the millions, or when Firebase Rulesa and Security will prevent access to some of the records.

It's now possible to iterate the list of products by only downloading a few bytes per product, quickly fetching metadata for displaying products in a UI.

After seeing the preceding flattern structure, if you are thinking that it is really okay to look up each record individually in Firebase, then yes it is, because Firebase internally uses web sockets and client libraries for incoming and outgoing requests for optimization. Even if we get tens of thousand records, this approach is still okay and perfectly reasonable.

> Always create the data structure that can scale in future when the app user grows.

Avoid arrays

The Firebase documentation has already mentioned and cleared this topic to avoid using arrays in Firebase Database, but I want to highlight some of the use cases where you can use the Arrays for storing the data.

Refer to the following points; if all the following are true, we can use Array to store the data in Firebase:

- If one client can write the data at a time
- For removing the keys, instead of using `.remove()`, we can save the array and splice it
- We need to take care when referring to anything by array index (a mutable key)

Date object

When we talk about sorting and filtering the data in Firebase with `created_date`, ensure that you have added the `created_date` key in every object that you have created along with date timestamp, such as `ref.set(new Date().toString())` and `ref.set(new Date().getTime())`, because Firebase has not supported JavaScript date object type (`ref.set(new Date());`).

Custom claims

Firebase Admin SDK provides the ability to add custom attributes in profile object; with the help of this, we can give user different access control, including role-based controls in the react-firebase app, so they are not designed to store additional data (such as profile and other custom data). We know that this looks like a very convenient way to do so, but it is strongly not recommended, as these claims are stored in the ID token and that impacts the performance issues, because all authenticated requests always contain a Firebase ID token corresponding to the signed in user.

- Custom claims are only for storing the data for controlling user access
- Custom claims are limited in size, so passing a custom claims greater than 1000 bytes will throw an error

Managing the user session

Manage the session for the user and give the prompt to reauthenticate, because every time when the user logged in, user credentials are sent to the Firebase Authentication backend and exchanged for a Firebase ID token (a JWT) and refresh token.

These are the common scenarios where we need to manage the session of the user:

- User is deleted
- User is disabled
- Email address and password changed

The Firebase Admin SDK also gives the ability to revoke the specific user session using the `revokeRefreshToken()` method. It revokes active refresh tokens of a given user. If we reset the password, Firebase Authentication backend automatically revokes the user token.

The following rule must be configured when any data requires authentication to access:

```
{
  "rules": {
  "users": {
  "$user_id": {
  ".read": "$user_id === auth.uid && auth.token.auth_time >
(root.child('metadata').child(auth.uid).child('revokeTime').val() || 0)",
   ".write": "$user_id === auth.uid && auth.token.auth_time >
(root.child('metadata').child(auth.uid).child('revokeTime').val() || 0)"
   }
  }
  }
}
```

Enabling offline capabilities in JavaScript

When we create Realtime Application with Firebase, we also need to monitor the connection when clients connect and disconnect with database. Firebase provides a simple solution, which you can use to write to the database when a client disconnects from the Firebase Database servers. We can perform all operations such as writing, setting, updating, and removing can be performed upon a disconnection.

Refer to this example `onDiscconnect()` method of Firebase:

```
var presenceRef = firebase.database().ref("disconnectmessage");
// Write the string when client loses connection
presenceRef.onDisconnect().set("I disconnected!");
```

We can also attach the callback function to ensure that the `onDisconnect()` method is attached properly:

```
presenceRef.onDisconnect().remove(function(err) {
  if (err) {
  console.error('onDisconnect event not attached properly', err);
  }
});
```

To cancel the `onDisconnect()` method, we can call `.cancel()` method `onDisconnectRef.cancel();`.

For detecting the connection state, Firebase Realtime Database provides special location `/.info/connected`.

This is updated every time app connection state changes; it returns the boolean value to check whether the client connection state is connected:

```
var connectedRef = firebase.database().ref(".info/connected");
connectedRef.on("value", function(snap) {
  if (snap.val() === true) {
  alert("connected");
  } else {
  alert("not connected");
  }
});
```

Optimize database performance

There are a few things where we also need to focus, such as Firebase Realtime Database performance in your app, to see how we can optimize your Realtime Database performance using different Realtime Database monitoring tools.

Monitor Realtime Database

We can collect the data of our Realtime Database's performance through a few different tools:

- **High-level overview:** We can use the Firebase profiler tool for a list of unindexed queries and a realtime overview of read/write operations. For using the profiler tool, ensure that you have installed Firebase CLI and run the following command.
- **Billed usage estimate:** FIrebase usage metrics provide you your billed usage and high-level performance metrics in Firebase Console.
- **Detailed drilldown:** Stackdriver Monitoring tool provides you with a more granular look at how your database is performing over time.

 For more details about profiling, visit `https://firebase.google.com/docs/database/usage/profile`

Improve performance by metric

Once you've gathered data, explore the following best practices and strategies based on the performance area you want to improve:

Metric	Description	Best practices
Load/Utilization	Optimize how much of your database's capacity is in use processing requests at any given time (reflected in **Load** or **io/database_load** metrics).	Optimize your data structure (https://firebase. google.com/docs/database/ usage/optimize#data-structure) Shared data across databases (https://firebase. google.com/docs/database/ usage/optimize#shard-data) Improve listener efficiency (https://firebase. google.com/docs/database/ usage/optimize#efficient-listeners) Limit downloads with query-based rules (https://firebase. google.com/docs/database/ usage/optimize#query-rules) Optimize connections (https:// firebase.google.com/docs/ database/usage/optimize#open-connections)
Active connections	Balance the number of simultaneous and active connections to your database to stay under the 100,000-connection limit.	Shard data across databases (https://firebase.google.com/ docs/database/usage/ optimize#shard-data) Reduce new connections (https:// firebase.google.com/docs/ database/usage/optimize#open-connections)

Outgoing bandwidth	If the downloads from your database seem higher than you want them to be, you can improve the efficiency of your read operations and reduce encryption overhead.	Optimize connections (`https://firebase.google.com/docs/database/usage/optimize#open-connections`) Optimize your data structure (`https://firebase.google.com/docs/database/usage/optimize#data-structure`) Limit downloads with query-based rules (`https://firebase.google.com/docs/database/usage/optimize#query-rules`) Reuse SSL sessions (`https://firebase.google.com/docs/database/usage/optimize#ssl-sessions`) Improve listener efficiency (`https://firebase.google.com/docs/database/usage/optimize#efficient-listeners`) Restrict access to data (`https://firebase.google.com/docs/database/usage/optimize#secure-data`)
Storage	Ensure that you're not storing unused data, or balance your stored data across other databases, and/or Firebase products to remain under quota.	Clean up unused data (`https://firebase.google.com/docs/database/usage/optimize#cleanup-storage`) Optimize your data structure (`https://firebase.google.com/docs/database/usage/optimize#data-structure`) Shard data across databases (`https://firebase.google.com/docs/database/usage/optimize#shard-data`) Use Firebase Storage (`https://firebase.google.com/docs/storage`)

Source: `https://firebase.google.com/docs/database/usage/optimize`

We can create multiple Realtime Database instances if we're using Blaze pricing plan; then, we can create multiple database instances in the same Firebase project.

To edit and deploy rules from the Firebase CLI, follow these steps:

```
firebase target:apply database main my-db-1 my-db-2
firebase target:apply database other my-other-db-3
Update firebase.json with the deploy targets:
{
"database": [
{"target": "main", "rules", "foo.rules.json"},
{"target": "other", "rules": "bar.rules.json"}
]
}

firebase deploy
```

Ensure that you consistently edit and deploy rules from the same place.

Connect your app to multiple database instances

Use the database reference to access data stored in secondary database instances. You can get the reference for a specific database instance by URL or app. If we don't specify a URL in the `.database()` method, then we'll get the reference for the app's default database instance:

```
// Get the default database instance for an app
var database = firebase.database();
// Get a secondary database instance by URL
var database =
firebase.database('https://reactfirebaseapp-9897.firebaseio.com');
```

To see the list of Firebase Sample Projects, visit `https://firebase.google.com/docs/samples/`.

To see the list of Firebase Libraries, refer to `https://firebase.google.com/docs/libraries/`.

You can also subscribe to the `https://www.youtube.com/channel/UCP4bf6IHJJQehibu6ai_ _cg` channel to get updated.

Best practices with React and Redux

Whenever we have components with dynamic functionality, data comes into the picture; the same way, in React, we have to deal with dynamic data, which seems easy but not every time.

Sounds confusing!

It is easy but sometimes tough because, in React components, it's easy to pass properties with many ways for building rendering tree from it, but there is not much clarity to update the view.

In the preceding chapters, this statement is clearly shown, so if you are still not clear, refer to those.

Use of Redux

As we know, in SPAs (single page applications), when we have to contract with state and time, it will be difficult to handgrip state over time. Here, Redux helps a lot, how? This is because, in a JavaScript application, Redux is handling two states: one is Data state and another is UI state, and it's a standard option for SPAs (single page applications). Moreover, bear in mind that Redux can be used with Angular or Jquery or React JavaScript libraries or frameworks.

Difference between Redux and Flux

Redux is a tool, whereas Flux is just a pattern that you can't use, like plug and play or download it. I'm not denying that Redux has some influence from the Flux pattern, but as we can't say, it 100% looks like Flux.
Let's go ahead to refer to a few differences.

Redux follows three guiding principles, as shown, which will also cover the difference between Redux and Flux:

1. **Single store approach:** We saw in the earlier diagrams that Store is pretending as an "intermediary" for all kind of state modifications within application and Redux. It is controlling direct communication between two components through the Store, a single point of communication. Here, the difference between Redux and Flux is that Flux has multiple store approaches and Redux has a single store approach.

2. **Read-Only State:** In React applications, components cannot change state directly, but they have to dispatch change to Store through "actions". Here, Store is an object, and it has four methods, as shown:

- store.dispatch(action)
- store.subscribe(listener)
- store.getState()
- replaceReducer(nextReducer)

3. **Reducer Functions to change the State:** Reducer function will handle dispatching actions to change the state as Redux tool doesn't allow direct communication between two components; so it will not only change the state but also, the dispatch action will be described for state change. Reducers here can be considered as pure-function. Here are a few characteristics to write reducer functions:

- No outside database or network calls
- Returns value based on its parameters
- Arguments are "immutable"
- The same argument returns the same value

Reducer functions are called pure-functions as they are purely doing nothing except returning a value based on their set parameters; it doesn't have any other consequences. They are recommended to have a flat state. In Flux or Redux architecture, it's always tough to deal with nested resources, which are from APIs' return, so it's been recommended to have a flat state in your component, such as normalize.

 Hint for pros: `const data = normalize(response, arrayOf(schema.user))   state = _.merge(state, data.entities)`

Immutable React State

In flat state, we have the benefit of dealing with nested resource and in the Immutable object, we have the benefit of a declared state that cannot be modified.

The other benefit of the Immutable object is that with their reference level equality checks, we can have fabulous improved rendering performance. In Immutable, we have an example of `shouldComponentUpdate`:

```
shouldComponentUpdate(nexProps) {
  // instead of object deep comparsion
  return this.props.immutableFoo !== nexProps.immutableFoo
}
```

In JavaScript, use of Immutability Deep freeze node will help you to freeze a node before mutation, and then it will verify results. The following example shows the same logic:

```
return {
  ...state,
  foo
}
return arr1.concat(arr2)
```

I hope that the preceding examples would have made things clear about immutable JS's use and benefits. It is also having a non-complicated way, but its use is very low:

```
import { fromJS } from 'immutable'
const state = fromJS({ bar: 'biz' })
const newState = foo.set('bar', 'baz')
```

From my point of view, it's very a fast and beautiful feature to be used.

React Routing

We have to use routing in client-side applications, and, for ReactJS also, we need one or the other routing library, so I recommend that you use react-router-dom instead of react-router.

Advantages:

- Views declaration in standardized structure help us to instantly understand what are our app views
- Using react-router-dom, we can easily handle the nested views and their progressive resolution of views
- Using browsing history feature user can navigate backward/forward and restore the state of view
- Dynamic Route matching
- CSS transitions on views when navigating
- Standardized app structure and behavior, useful when working in a team

Note: React router doesn't provide any way to handle data-fetching. We need to use async-props or other React data fetching mechanism.

It's been seen that very few developers who are dealing with webpack know about code splitting of your application code in several files of JavaScript:

```
require.ensure([], () => {
  const Profile = require('./Profile.js')
  this.setState({
    currentComponent: Profile
  })
})
```

This split of code is necessary because each code is not useful to each user, and it's not necessary to load that chunk of code in each page, which will be a burden for the browser, so to avoid such a situation, we should split our application into several chunks.

Now, you will have a question like if we will have more chunks of code, we will have to have more HTTP requests and that will also affect performance, but with the help of HTTP/2multiplexed, your problem will be resolved. You can also combine your chunked code with chunk hashing, which will also optimize your browser cache ratio whenever you change your code.

JSX components

JSX is nothing, but, in simple words, it is just an extension of JavaScript syntax. Also, if you observe the syntax or structure of JSX, you will find that it's similar to XML coding. JSX is doing preprocessor footstep, which adds XML syntax to JavaScript. Though you can certainly use React without JSX, JSX makes react a lot more neat and elegant. Similar to XML, JSX tags are having tag name, attributes, and children and, in that, if an attribute value is enclosed in quotes, that value becomes a string.

JSX works similar to XML, with balanced opening and closing tags, and it helps make large trees at ease to read than "function calls" or "object literals".

Advantages of using JSX in React:

- JSX is very simple to understand and think about than JavaScript functions
- Markup of JSX is more acquainted to designer and the rest of your team
- Your markup becomes more semantic, structured and more meaningful

How is it easy to visualize?

As I said, the structure/syntax is easy to visualize/notice, which is intended to be more clear and readable in the JSX format as compared to JavaScript.

Semantics / structured syntax

In our applications, we can see how JSX syntax is easy to understand and visualize; behind this, there is a big reason of having semantic syntax structure. JSX, with pleasure, converts your JavaScript code into more semantic and meaningful structured markup. This consents you the benefit of declaring your component structure and information pour using an HTML-like syntax, knowing that it will transform into simple JavaScript functions. React outlines all the HTML elements you would expect in the React.DOM namespace. The good part is that it also allows you to use your own written, custom components within the markup.

Use of PropType in React component

In a React component, we can pass the properties from higher-level component, so knowledge of properties is a must, as it will give you more flexibility to extend your component and saves your time:

```
MyComponent.propTypes = {
  isLoading: PropTypes.bool.isRequired,
  items: ImmutablePropTypes.listOf(
    ImmutablePropTypes.contains({
      name: PropTypes.string.isRequired,
    })
  ).isRequired
}
```

You can also validate your properties the way we can validate properties of Immutable JS with react immutable proptypes.

Benefit of higher-order components

Higher-order components are nothing but extended versions of your original component:

```
PassData({ foo: 'bar' })(MyComponent)
```

The main benefit of using them is that we can use it in multiple situations, for example, authentication or login validation:

```
requireAuth({ role: 'admin' })(MyComponent)
```

The other benefit is that with higher-order components, you can fetch data separately and set your logic to have your views in a simple way.

Redux Architecture benefits

Compared to other frameworks, it has more plus points:

1. It might not have any other way effects.
2. As we know, binding is not needed because components can't interact directly.
3. States are managed globally, so less possibility of mismanagement.
4. Sometimes, for middleware, it would be difficult to manage other way effects.

From the mentioned points, it's very clear that the Redux architecture is very powerful, and it has reusability as well.

 We can also use build React-Firebase application with the **ReactFire** library, with a few lines of JavaScript. We can integrate Firebase data into React apps via ReactFireMixin.

Summary

In this last and final chapter of this book, we covered the best practices to be followed when working with React and Firebase. We also saw how we can monitor application performance with the use of different tools to reduce the number of bugs. We also talked about the importance of the structure of your data in Firebase Realtime database and discussed the dynamic data passing to React components. We also looked at other key factors, such as JSX, React Routing, and React PropTypes, which are the topmost usable elements in React App. We also learned that Redux helps a lot in maintaining the state of your **Single Page Applications (SPAs)**.

Other Books You May Enjoy

If you enjoyed this book, you may be interested in these other books by Packt:

React 16 Essentials - Second Edition
Artemij Fedosejev, Adam Boduch

ISBN: 978-1-78712-604-6

- Learn to code React 16 with hands-on examples and clear tutorials
- Install powerful React 16 tools to make development much more efficient
- Understand the impact of React Fiber today and the future of your web development
- Utilize the Redux application architecture with your React components
- Create React 16 elements with properties and children
- Get started with stateless and stateful React components
- Use JSX to speed up your React 16 development process
- Add reactivity to your React 16 components with lifecycle methods
- Test your React 16 components with the Jest test framework

React Native Blueprints
Emilio Rodriguez Martinez

ISBN: 978-1-78728-809-6

- Structure React Native projects to ease maintenance and extensibility
- Optimize a project to speed up development
- Make a React Native project production-ready
- Use external modules to speed up the development and maintenance of your projects
- Explore the different UI and code patterns to be used for iOS and Android
- Get to know the best practices when building apps in React Native

Leave a review - let other readers know what you think

Please share your thoughts on this book with others by leaving a review on the site that you bought it from. If you purchased the book from Amazon, please leave us an honest review on this book's Amazon page. This is vital so that other potential readers can see and use your unbiased opinion to make purchasing decisions, we can understand what our customers think about our products, and our authors can see your feedback on the title that they have worked with Packt to create. It will only take a few minutes of your time, but is valuable to other potential customers, our authors, and Packt. Thank you!

Index